ECONOMIC INTEGRATION:
THE EAST AFRICAN EXPERIENCE

Studies in the Economics of Africa

Editors: I. LIVINGSTONE and H. W. ORD

Money and Credit in Developing Africa
ERIC L. FURNESS

Economic Integration:
The East African Experience
ARTHUR HAZLEWOOD

Economic Integration: The East African Experience

ARTHUR HAZLEWOOD

Senior Research Officer
Institute of Economics and Statistics, Oxford
Fellow of Pembroke College

HEINEMANN

LONDON · NAIROBI · IBADAN · LUSAKA

Heinemann Educational Books Ltd
48 Charles Street, London W1X 8AH
P.M.B. 5205 Ibadan · P.O. Box 45314 Nairobi
P.O. Box 3966 Lusaka

EDINBURGH MELBOURNE TORONTO AUCKLAND
SINGAPORE HONG KONG KUALA LUMPUR NEW DELHI

ISBN 0 435 84402 4 (Cased)
     0 435 84403 2 (Paper)

First published 1975

Printed in Great Britain by Richard Clay (The Chaucer Press), Ltd,
Bungay, Suffolk

Contents

Preface

Since I first became interested in the subject of this book, some fifteen years ago, I have had the advantage of working from time to time in various branches of the East African Community and its predecessor, and in the Kenya Government; I have also benefited from association with the East African universities. My chief debt is to the East Africans and expatriates, too numerous to mention individually, from whom I have learned on these occasions. I am indebted to the editors and publishers of the *Bulletin of the Oxford University Institute of Economics and Statistics*, the *East African Economic Review*, the East African Statistical Department's *Economic and Statistical Review*, and the *Standard Bank Review* for permission to use material originally published by them, and to Chatham House for allowing me to draw on two chapters I contributed to *African Integration and Disintegration* (Oxford University Press for Chatham House, 1967). I have benefited from comments on parts of a draft of the book from Gordon Harris, Ian Livingstone, Alison Smith, and Robert Stevens. They are not responsible for the faults that remain where I have ignored their advice. I am grateful to Mary Gisborne and Sally Lay for fast and accurate typing.

A.H.

Oxford, January 1975

A Note on Currency Units

The currency unit in East Africa is the shilling. An East African shilling for use in all three countries was issued by the East African Currency Board until separate central banks were established in the 1960s, which issued their own shillings, officially at par with each other. It was usual for large values to be expressed in £s (£1 = shs. 20/–), and this practice is retained in Kenya. In the other countries, and in the East African Community, the use of the £ has been abandoned and all values are expressed in shillings. It would have been artificial to convert all past figures, originally expressed in £s, into shillings, and it would have been inappropriate to convert all recent figures into £s. Figures have therefore generally been given in the units in which they were originally expressed, though conversion has been necessary where a table includes years which span the change in practice.

List of Tables

List of Maps

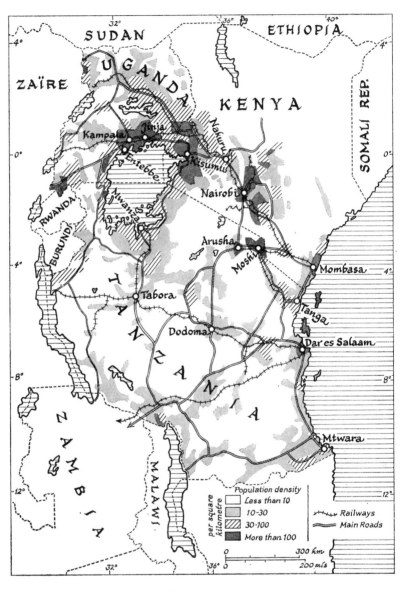

I. *Kenya, Tanzania and Uganda*

1 Introduction

The three East African countries, Kenya, Tanzania* and Uganda, occupy an area of 680,000 square miles (1·8 m. sq. km) stretching for some 800 miles (1,300 km) from the Indian Ocean to the Ruwenzori Mountains and the Great Lakes in the west, and for over 1,000 miles (1,600 km) southwards from the borders of Ethiopia and the Sudan to Mozambique. In addition, the three East African countries also border on Somalia, Zaïre, Burundi, Rwanda, and Zambia. The area of Kenya, Uganda, and Tanzania embraces a wide variety of geographical conditions, in terms of altitude, temperature, and rainfall, which affect the distribution of population and the character and location of economic activity. The population is unevenly distributed over the area, as may be most easily seen from Map 1. In particular, the population of Kenya is in three clusters, at the Coast, in the central highlands, and around Lake Victoria, with parts of the north and east virtually unpopulated, while in Tanzania the clusters of population are widely separated and dispersed around the periphery of the country.

There were links between the different peoples of East Africa and between East Africans and the outside world long before the Europeans set off on their venture to the interior in the last decades of the nineteenth century. The population distribution at that time was the result of great movements of people over eastern Africa which had taken place in the past and were continuing. The peoples of East Africa were not static, nor were they isolated. There was trade with the coast and within the interior, carried on by Africans as well as later by Arabs, and not only in ivory, guns and slaves.[1] There was, however, little in geography or pre-colonial history to define the boundaries of East Africa as an economic or political unit, or those of the three countries within it. That definition had its origins primarily in the colonial experience.

*Tanzania was formed by the union of Tanganyika (now Mainland Tanzania) and Zanzibar in April 1964.

British interest in East Africa was initially centred on Uganda, which came under British administration in the 1890s. This interest led to the construction of the Uganda Railway from the East African coast to Lake Victoria. Construction was started in 1896, and at the end of 1901 the line reached the Lake, which until 1902 (together with much of the western part of what is now Kenya) was included in Uganda. With the construction of the railway East Africa began to take on its modern shape. The railway not only made possible the development of the export trade of Uganda, it also made practicable and provided an important incentive for the encouragement of European settlement in Kenya, as a way of providing development and traffic along the line of rail. With the growth of the settler community, Kenya began to acquire a dominant position in East African affairs.

German administration spread over what is now mainland Tanzania from the late 1880s, and was replaced by the British after the first world war when Tanganyika became a Mandated Territory under the League of Nations. From then until Independence was achieved between 1961 and 1963, the three countries were under the administration of the same colonial power, which was a fundamental factor in the establishment of the common institutions and arrangements with which this book is concerned, and in their development on an *ad hoc* basis without a formal constitutional framework.

Although all three countries were under British administration, their economic development during the colonial period did not conform to a single pattern. The monetary economy of Uganda developed on the basis of production by African farmers, particularly of cotton and coffee. There were few estates and few settlers. In Tanganyika, estate production, particularly of sisal, African farmers' production of coffee and cotton, and European mixed farming all became important in the monetary economy. In Kenya the structure of the money economy was to a major extent determined by the existence of relatively large numbers of European settlers. In Kenya a substantial part of the agricultural output in the monetary economy was produced on European-owned farms and was for domestic consumption, whereas African monetary agriculture, which predominated in the other territories, and particularly in Uganda, was largely for export. In Kenya, agricultural production for the monetary economy was carried out by wage labour rather than by small farmers. Kenya was less export-oriented than the other territories, the value of exports being a less important determinant of money income than in Uganda and Tanzania. On the other hand Kenya was a larger importer. Kenya's deficit on external trade was to a significant extent offset by surpluses in her trade with Tanganyika and Uganda, and her exports to them increasingly came to consist of manufactures. The imported content of Kenya's inter-territorial exports was one reason for her large imports, though more important were the effects of the high propensity to import by Europeans and other high-income residents and the inflow of capital. Kenya was an important entrepôt. The transport routes brought almost all Uganda's foreign trade through Kenya, and also a good deal of that of the Lake Province and the Northern Province of Tanganyika. It was not only transit trade. A large value of the imports of the other territories was handled by Kenya merchants. In 1949 only 20 per cent of Uganda's imports were consigned directly to Uganda, though the proportion had risen to 55 per cent by 1960, in which year three-quarters of Tanganyika's imports were directly consigned.

Agriculture was a less important component of the monetary economy in Kenya than in Uganda or Tanganyika, but services and manufacturing were more developed. Administration and commerce were more highly developed in Kenya than elsewhere in East Africa, and there was also a highly developed system of agricultural marketing and processing (for example the Kenya Dairy Board and Kenya Co-operative Creameries), primarily directed to serve the European farmers. Asians played a leading part in commerce and the professions in all three territories, but they were more numerous in Kenya than elsewhere, and this added to the economic effects of the European population.

These influences on the structure of the Kenya economy were reinforced by the development of Kenya as a supplier of both goods and services to the whole of East Africa. This is a matter which is a major theme of this book. At this point it is necessary only to remark that to companies operating throughout East Africa the capital of Kenya, Nairobi, appeared the natural location for their headquarters. In a similar fashion it appeared the natural location for most of the headquarters of the various inter-territorial services that were established. The effect was cumulative, because the growth of Nairobi, originally a railway construction camp, as the commercial and administrative capital of East Africa, increased the number of European and other high-income residents and further reinforced its 'natural' attractions.

If the outcome of the structure of the East African economies that has been described is measured in terms of national income aggregates – and the available figures must be taken at best as indicating only broad orders of magnitude – the income per head in Kenya appears markedly higher than in the other territories. But Kenya must not be seen as a rich 'centre' surrounded by a poor 'periphery'. The higher income per head in Kenya was the arithmetical consequence of the larger number of non-Africans. In general, African incomes in Kenya were no higher than elsewhere in East Africa, and almost certainly lower than in some parts of Uganda. In fact, there was a flow of labour out of Kenya to the rest of East Africa, particularly to Uganda. What must be emphasized is that in all three countries the great bulk of the

TABLE 1.1

Area and population, 1961

	Kenya		Tanganyika		Uganda	
Area, 1000 sq. miles (1000 sq. km.)						
Land	220	(569)	341	(884)	75	(197)
Water	5	(13)	21	(53)	16	(39)
Total	225	(583)	362	(937)	91	(237)
Population per sq. mile (sq. km.) of land area	38·0	(14·7)	27·6	(10·7)	91·3	(34·7)
Population ('000)						
Africans	8,082		9,281		6,751	
Europeans	59		23		12	
Asians and others	211		117		82	
Total	8,352		9,421		6,845	
Approximate proportion of total population living in towns, per cent	7		3		2	

Source: EASD, *Economic and Statistical Review.*

TABLE 1.2

Estimated population, 1973

	'000
Kenya	12,482
Tanzania (mainland)	13,974
Uganda	10,810

Source: EASD, *Economic and Statistical Review.*

TABLE 1.3

Gross domestic product (monetary and non-monetary)

	Average 1961–3			1971		
	Kenya	Tanganyika	Uganda	Kenya	Tanzania	Uganda
Total GDP, £m.	243	212	163	576	442	469
of which per cent:						
Primary production	42	62	65	32	41	55
Manufacturing	10	4	4	13	10	8
Construction	3	3	2	5	5	2
Services	46	32	29	51	44	35

Sources: 1961–3, Van Arkadie, B., and Ghai, D., 'The East African Economies', *The Economies of Africa*, Robson, P., and Lury, D. A., eds. (London: George Allen and Unwin, 1969), p. 321; 1971, EASD, *Economic and Statistical Review*.

TABLE 1.4

Gross domestic product, 1971

	Kenya	Tanzania	Uganda
Non-monetary			
Total GDP shs. m.	2,538	2,573	3,159
of which per cent:			
Primary production	80	74	91
Construction	8	3	1
Services	12	23	8
Monetary			
Total GPD shs. m.	8,978	6,273	6,211
of which per cent:			
Primary production	18	27	37
Manufacturing	16	14	13
Construction	4	7	2
Services	62	52	48

Source: EASD, *Economic and Statistical Review*.

TABLE 1.5

Income per capita, 1962

	£s		
	Kenya	Tanganyika	Uganda
African, monetary	7	8	10
African, total	15	16	17
Non-African	400	371	291

Source: Van Arkadie and Ghai, op. cit., p. 324.

TABLE 1.6

Share of small farms in monetary agriculture

per cent					
Kenya		Tanzania		Uganda	
1960	20	1960–2 av.	58	1960	80
1972	52	1968	74	1970	77

Sources: Kenya, gross marketed production, *Economic Survey*, 1973 and 1966. Tanzania, net output of private agriculture, *Annual Economic Survey*, 1968. Uganda, value of main cash-crops, *Statistical Abstract*, 1971. Coffee, cotton, tobacco assumed produced on small farms, and tea and sugar-cane on estates.

TABLE 1.7

Exports as percentage of gross domestic product

	1962	1971
Kenya	21	16
Tanzania	37	28
Uganda	35	27

Source: EASD, *Economic and Statistical Review*.

TABLE 1.8

External and inter-territorial trade

	£m.		
	Kenya	Tanzania	Uganda
1961			
External			
Exports	41·7	50·6	41·3
Imports	68·9	39·7	26·5
Balance	−27·2	+10·9	+14·8
Inter-territorial			
Exports	15·9	2·2	6·9
Imports	7·0	10·6	7·4
Balance	+9·0	−8·4	−0·5
Total			
Balance	−18·2	+2·5	+14·3
1971			
External			
Exports	78·4	89·6	84·0
Imports	184·1	120·7	68·1
Balance	−105·7	−31·1	+15·9
Inter-territorial			
Exports	33·9	9·9	8·9
Imports	16·0	15·6	21·1
Balance	+17·9	−5·7	−12·2
Total			
Balance	−87·8	−36·8	+3·7

Note: Exports = domestic exports + re-exports.

Source: *Annual Trade Reports.*

TABLE 1.9

Source of main tax revenues

(Per cent of East African total)

	Kenya		Tanzania		Uganda	
	1960	1970	1960	1970	1960	1970
Import duties	45	48	31	30	24	22
Excise duties	42	43	29	30	29	27
Income tax	60	58	20	25	20	17

Source: EASD, *Economic and Statistical Review.*

TABLE 1.10

Indicators of relative economic size

	1961			1972		
	Kenya	Tanganyika	Uganda	Kenya	Tanzania	Uganda
Goods handled at main harbours, ('000 tons)	3,407	1,352	n.a.	5,893	3,387	n.a.
Passengers at main airports ('000)	391	99	106	1,132	300	360
Sales of motor spirit (m. gall.)	33	19	17	64	34	30
Assets of commercial banks, end year (£m.)	60	30	21	253	183	111
P.O. Savings bank balances, end year (£m.)	6·5	1·5	1·5	5·8	2·7	n.a.
Government revenue (£m.)	41	29	19	179	168	78

Notes: Tanganyika (Tanzania) harbours: Dar es Salaam and Tanga; Kenya harbour: Mombasa (Mombasa harbour serves Kenya and Uganda and part of northern Tanzania, though the 1972 figure may be influenced by attempts to direct more Tanzanian traffic through Tanzanian harbours).

n.a. = not available or not applicable.

Source: EASD, *Economic and Statistical Review.*

population consisted of African farmers producing largely for their own subsistence.

The statistics in Tables 1.1 to 1.10 illustrate some of these characteristics of the East African economies at the end of the colonial period. They also show the situation after ten years of independence. There were certainly changes over the decade. Notably, the importance of European agriculture in Kenya was greatly diminished, with the transformation of many farms into African smallholdings, and with the expansion of cash-crop production in traditional African areas. But also noticeable is the extent to which Kenya maintained its position in the East African economy.

NOTE

[1] For the pre-colonial situation see, for example, Smith, A., 'The Southern Section of the Interior, 1840–84' in Oliver, R., and Mathew, G. (eds), *History of East Africa*, Vol. I (Oxford: Clarendon Press, 1963).

2 Benefits and Problems of Economic Integration [1]

Economic integration in East Africa developed over the decades without benefit of theory. It was a pragmatic response to administrative and commercial needs. However, there is a substantial body of economic theory concerning customs unions,[2] and although this theory may not be of much relevance to less-developed countries, an analysis in general terms of the benefits and problems of economic integration may assist an understanding of the East African experience.

In broad outline, the argument of the conventional theory is that a customs union will be beneficial if on balance it is 'trade-creating', and it will be harmful if on balance it is 'trade-diverting'. The removal of tariffs on intra-union trade will tend to increase trade between the countries forming the union. Whether or not the union is beneficial will depend on whether the intra-union trade is on balance the result of trade creation or of trade diversion.

If union causes a member to replace its own high-cost production of particular commodities with imports from other members of the union which have lower costs, this is trade-creating. This trade creation is likely when there is union between countries which produce much the same range of products but differ in their comparative advantage for the various products. Before union, such countries are actually competitive but potentially complementary. After union, competition will lead to a pattern of specialization in which each country produces and supplies to the other members of the union the products in which it has a comparative advantage. The high-cost industries in each country will tend to be displaced by their low-cost competitors in other members of the union. Through the creation of intra-union trade, each member will be supplied from the lowest-cost source within the union.

If, on the other hand, the effect of union is to cause members to switch their purchases from low-cost external sources to high-cost sources within the union, there is trade diversion. Union will not have been beneficial because it will have caused a shift of resources into less efficient uses.

Trade creation is likely to be predominant in unions between countries where a small proportion of total expenditure is on external trade, and where a high proportion of that external trade takes place between the countries which are to form the union. The less important the external trade with non-union countries, the smaller will be the effect of union in diverting imports to higher-cost sources within the union. The more important the domestic trade in total expenditure, the more the union is likely to create intra-union trade by displacing high-cost domestic production.

The countries of East Africa, in common with those of other groupings of less-developed countries, do not satisfy these requirements for a beneficial customs union. External trade is relatively large, and intra-union trade relatively small. The benefits arising from a redistribution in the pattern of production within the union, given the under-developed nature of the economies and the importance of primary production for export, would not be large, and for some members could be negative. If a case is to be made out for a customs union of countries similar to those of East Africa it must be based not on the effect of union in achieving a more efficient utilization of existing productive resources, but on the stimulus it gives to economic growth. Such a case can be based on the larger market provided by a customs union, which will enable productive enterprises, particularly in manufacturing, to obtain economies of scale. The benefits will accrue partly in the form of a more efficient scale of operation by existing enterprises, but primarily from a greater rate of investment in new industries. In addition, there are possibly benefits to be gained from specialization between countries within the common market according to comparative advantage.

For these effects of a customs union to be counted as benefits it is not necessary first to argue the case for protection. The point is that for any given level of protection, industries will operate more efficiently and at lower cost if they are able to serve a wider market area created by the customs union than if they are restricted to the market of a single country. The argument for integration is that so long as there are economies of scale to be obtained, or so long as there are possibilities for specialization between countries on the lines of comparative advantage, industrialization to serve the wider regional market will be more efficient than industrialization within the confines of each national market.

Given the frequent similarity between the resource endowments of different underdeveloped countries, it is probable that the second basis for the argument is not a particularly strong one. The argument for integration, therefore, hangs on the assumption that the size of the market is of predominant importance for industrialization. This is an assumption that requires some examination.

In assessing the importance of economies of scale to a particular industry it is not enough to look at the size of the market in relation to the technical economies of scale, including the economies of intra-industry specialization. Even if the national market is large enough to provide these economies to a particular industry, there could still be gains from the enlargement of the market. In a larger market more than one producer might be able to achieve the technical economies of scale, so that there could be the additional economies arising from competition between them. Of course, a market of this size is not a sufficient condition for the benefits of competition between technically optimum-sized plants to be achieved, and the existence of more than one producer does not guarantee that they will compete. But to obtain the potential benefits of competition a market which is a multiple of that required for the technical economies is necessary.

Furthermore, there are likely to be cases where the technical economies of scale cannot be obtained by more than a single plant, and perhaps not by that, even within the integrated market. And it must not be taken for granted that competition between a number of small firms will give results preferable to those resulting from a monopoly of a technically superior firm. But the danger that the benefits of economies of scale might be offset by a monopoly position of the producer should be a warning against too high an external tariff.

It may be the case that a product is already being produced in more than one of the countries forming the union. The removal of tariffs between the members may then result in competition that increases efficiency and results in one of the plants expanding, and reaping economies of scale, at the expense of the others. It is not obvious, however, that such a process, which involves the destruction of some existing industries, is desirable in very under-industrialized countries.

Economies of scale might be obtained within an integrated area by intra-industry specialization, in which the process of production is divided up between specialist producers. There could also be inter-industry specialization agreements between the members; this specialization between countries would require an agreed investment policy and would come near to requiring a common plan for the whole integrated area.

Economies of scale vary greatly from industry to industry. But there can be little doubt that the East African countries are sufficiently small for many industries to be able to operate more efficiently if given access to the whole East African market than if confined to the market of a single country.

Of course, integration is not simply a matter of the absence of tariffs. The harmonization of a range of economic policies is usually thought to be necessary if the customs union is to operate as a single, unified market. Of the greatest importance in the case of less-developed countries is the establishment of infra-structure – transport facilities and commercial organization – without which intra-union trade will not develop, even in the absence of tariffs. East Africa, in fact, is better off in this respect than most, if not all, groupings of less-developed countries, with railway and high-quality road links between the three members of the common market. Indeed, in a sense the transport links have been too good, and this has led to the creation of artificial barriers to reduce the competitiveness of Kenyan industry in Tanzania and Uganda. The point about the importance of transport in the establishment of an effective customs union comes into its own, however, in connection with any widening of the East African union to include neighbouring countries.

The most difficult problems of a customs union arise from the fact that it is likely to affect different members differently. The purpose of establishing the preferential area is to switch the purchases of the members away from goods imported from the outside world to goods produced within the union. If the establishment of the preference were necessary to secure this switch, a loss will have been imposed on the member countries.

This loss is sometimes seen in fiscal terms: goods which previously carried a customs duty are now obtained from within the union and the customs revenue is lost. But it is more than a fiscal problem. The loss could equally take the form of higher domestic prices, because purchasing has been switched from imports from the outside world to higher-priced goods produced within the union. Most likely there would be a combination of revenue loss and higher prices – but these are not separate and distinct losses; they are both reflections of the fact that there has been a switch from a low-cost to a higher-cost source of production.

This loss arises for a particular country just as much if it switches to its own domestic production as if it switches to products of other members of the union. But in another way there is a world of difference between these two situations. If the switch is to domestic products, to set against the losses there are the benefits of increased domestic production and economic activity. If the switch is to the goods of another member of the union, these production benefits go elsewhere. The losses are borne for the benefit of another country.

There would be no general problem (there would be problems for individual producers) if a country's losses on some products were offset by its gains on others. It could happen that a particular member of the union switched its purchases of some goods to other members of the union, while other members were switching their purchases of some other goods to itself. It would then gain on the swings what it lost on the roundabouts.

Unfortunately, it is unlikely that what may be called a '*laissez faire* union', in which no attempt is made to 'regulate' market forces in the interest of balanced development, would work in this way. The benefits are more likely to be rather unevenly distributed. There is likely to be a tendency for development to be polarized in a few members of the union. Some members will find the demand for their products rising while others – often because they do not produce very much that could benefit from intra-union trade – will find that they are increasing their purchases from other members of the union (with the consequent disadvantages of loss of revenue and higher prices) while they are themselves selling very little to the other members of the union. This situation will reinforce itself, because the former group will tend to attract investment and the latter group will not.

It is this tendency for the polarization of development in some members of the union which is the greatest obstacle to the viability of a *laissez faire* union. Development will tend to take place mainly in the countries which, for one reason or another, are the most attractive for industrial investment. The clustering of industry will generally be associated with and reinforced by disequalizing movements of capital and labour. The cumulative causation, which is an important feature of the development process, reinforces and increases the divergences between the relatively advanced and relatively backward members of the customs union.

An unequal distribution of the benefits of integration is not inevitable, but it is particularly likely to occur when the union is between countries of substantially different levels of development. The attractions of the established centre are a powerful influence towards the polarization of development in some parts of the union. The disequalizing tendencies will be increased where the less-developed countries do not, or cannot, produce goods which are demanded by the more developed. In this situation there will be little 'spill-over' of development from the more- to the less-developed members of the area. The losses imposed on the less-developed members may be relative or absolute. Some countries may merely obtain less of the growth than the others; but it is even possible that they would grow more rapidly outside than inside the union.

A *laissez faire* union in which the benefits are very unequally distributed is unlikely to survive for long. The uneven development of the different regions of a unitary state is not without its political difficulties. How much greater will be the difficulties of integration between independent states, each politically committed to a policy of development, if economic growth concentrates in some of them while others remain backwaters. The 'strains within the common market'[3] will become too strong. The arrangements will not take the strain – they will break. The weaker countries will come to believe (even if wrongly) that it would be better for them to go it alone. This is why it is unrealistic to emphasize the benefits to be gained in the aggregate from a common market, while neglecting the question of their distribution. Beyond a certain point, the very existence of the gains may depend on their tolerable distribution.

Nevertheless, it is important that recognition should be given to the fact that the quest for equality can be pushed too far. Inequalities within an economic union will not be solely caused by union. Without the union the various countries would have developed unequally, and too determined a pursuit of equality within the union could result in a generally slower rate of growth. And if a slow-growing country is small the scope for development within its national boundaries will be so limited that it would be unlikely to grow faster outside the union.

In principle, if there are gains in the aggregate to be had from integration it will be possible for every participant to be better off than it would be on its own. This is not to say that governments will always recognize the fact that there are benefits from union. One trouble is that no one knows what the rate of growth would be outside the union; it is much easier to see that other members are growing faster than oneself. Governments are particularly liable to ignore the benefits of union where the major gains are to be reaped only in the longer run.

The effect of the disequalizing tendencies on the viability of a *laissez faire* union point to the need for regulation, but it is not easy for the more advanced countries to accept the restrictions which would result from any regulation of the union. It is always likely that it will appear to the advanced country that it would do better to exert its competitive power in the attraction of new industries than to accept the constraints imposed by the rules of a regulated market. Nevertheless, it is difficult to believe that there is much future in *laissez faire* unions. The disequalizing forces are likely to be sufficiently powerful for such unions to be unacceptable to the weaker countries. If the aggregate gains from integration are large enough, there is always the possibility in a regulated union of attaining a distribution of the benefits under which all countries clearly feel themselves to be better off than in isolation. The hope for economic integration appears to lie, therefore, with regulated integration in which the gains can be seen to be large, and in which an acceptable distribution of the benefits has been achieved.

In what ways can an economic union be 'regulated' to make it acceptable to all members? The simplest form of regulation is the payment of fiscal compensation for the inequitable operation of the market. Within a unitary state, particularly if the tax system is progressive, there will almost inevitably be an automatic fiscal transfer to the benefit of the less economically favoured areas. In the rich areas central tax revenues will tend to exceed, and in the poor areas to fall short of, the level of expenditure, so that the rich areas subsidize the poor. Much the same effect is likely to arise in a federation, and there will tend to be automatic fiscal compensations for the disequalizing effects of the market. In an economic union in which there is no political association, and hence no common system of public finance, the automatic fiscal redistribution will be lacking. For the weaker countries, such a union gives the worst of both worlds. If fiscal transfers are to be used in such a union to compensate the losers, special arrangements must be devised.

There is every reason to believe, however, that fiscal transfers by themselves are an inadequate 'regulator'. Countries want revenue, but they also want development. In principle there must be some level of fiscal transfer which would 'compensate' for a lack of development, or would make it possible to develop by financing infra-structure, subsidies to industry, or other means. In practice, such a level is unlikely to be achievable. It might be guessed that the transfers needed to make the loser think it was compensated would in most cases be larger than the aggregate gains from integration. At any rate, they would need to be larger than the payer would accept. No doubt there is an illogicality in these attitudes, but they none the less speak decisively against the adequacy of a system of fiscal transfers as a regulator of a common market.

It is an inconvenient fact that other regulators are far more difficult to devise and to operate. They are also liable to be restrictionist, reducing the level of intra-union trade and the benefits of the common market. They may hinder or prevent the most efficient location of industry and deter some investment altogether. A system of fiscal redistribution does not directly attempt to affect the location of economic activity: it is concerned to redistribute its fruits. With some other regulatory measures the dilemma of equity or efficiency is sharper. To foster an equitable distribution of industry between the countries, should governments prevent some industries from locating themselves where they would be most efficient, which would usually be in the already most-developed areas? Almost certainly the answer must be: Yes, but not with a complete disregard of the cost. In assessing the cost it must be borne in mind that the internal economies of scale deriving from the size of the market may not be realized in the absence of the external economies associated with large industrial complexes. Even when an industry has free access to a large market, it may be unable to operate efficiently in an isolated location remote from a major industrial centre.

The most obviously restrictionist form of regulation would be the erection of barriers to intra-market trade in order to protect the industries of the weaker members against competition from those of the stronger. Such measures could have a part to play in a viable economic union, but if carried too far they become the negation of the common-market principle.

Less restrictionist would be an arrangement for the more backward countries to offer inducements to industry which the other members of the union agreed to forgo. The inducements could be fiscal, in the form of various tax exemptions. The trouble with most inducements of this kind is that they deprive the country offering them of revenue. The less-developed members of the union could ill afford this loss of revenue, particularly as their concessions might have to be very great if their disadvantages for industry were to be significantly reduced. In addition to fiscal inducements, more direct means could be adopted to increase the relative attractiveness of the more backward countries. An attempt could be made to build up their infra-structure. But the poverty of the backward countries will make it difficult for them to finance the necessary investments, and it would be unreasonable to suppose that the other countries would agree to refrain from further developing their own infra-structure.

Despite the difficulties, differential inducements could play a part in a regional development policy. A regional development policy – supranational planning, in other words – is of course the best answer to the problem of regulating a common market. It is an answer which occurs to most students of the problem. Unfortunately, it is not an entirely helpful answer, because the difficulties in the way of supranational planning are at least as great as those difficulties of the common market to which it is offered as a solution. The fundamental difficulty, of course, is the surrender of autonomy which is involved.

At the minimum of supranational planning is the 'confrontation' of national plans in the expectation that inconsistencies will be revealed and that action will be taken to eliminate them. Doubtless, inconsistencies would be revealed by such a confrontation, but if it is a confrontation of published plans, action is unlikely to follow. Though the targets of the plan may not be achieved (and inconsistencies with the plans of others may be one reason), it may be easier to face the problems of failure than the problems of radically changing the plan, particularly if this involves abandoning the attempt to establish some industries which feature in it.

A reconciliation of plans before they are completed goes much further than the confrontation of published plans. What such a reconciliation would amount to – if it did not go so far as to result in effect in the construction of a single, joint plan – would be an agreement on the allocation of particular industries for which free access to a market wider than that of any one of the countries was important. A list of industries would be drawn up and it would be agreed which country should have which industry.

Such an allocation procedure has often been suggested. The minimum necessary condition is that there shall be enough industries to go round. A list which was too short to provide at least one industry for each country could not be acceptable. Even a longer list may not be acceptable if the allocation of industries is markedly unequal. What is needed is a long list of industries so that each country can have a large absolute addition to its industry while, if necessary, the less-developed countries are allocated more than the rest. The difficulty with this solution is that allocation of a long list of industries is likely to be an exercise of some futility. Any list is an expression of hope – of hope that the industries can be attracted at all, and that they can be attracted to the countries to which they have been allocated. The longer the list the more 'hopeful' it becomes, and the more remote its full realization. But a long list, the realization of large parts of which is remote, is nothing more than a short list with all the difficulties of bargaining that are entailed in the allocation of a few industries.

Despite the difficulties of industrial allocation it is not a device which should be dismissed as a possible ingredient of a regulated customs union. No doubt some agreements can be reached on particular allocations. But it would be wrong to think of industrial allocation as a simple answer to the problem of the disequalizing tendencies of customs unions.

In determining the allocation of industries the dilemma between equity and efficiency is sharply raised, and it is in implementing the agreed allocation that differential inducements to industry have a part to play. But there can be no guarantee of their effectiveness, and it is likely to be smallest where regard has been paid in the allocation to equity rather than efficiency. Inducements offered by the country to which an industry has been allocated will need to be backed up by prohibiting the industry from being located in the territory of another member of the union. The danger is that the industry will not be established at all, and adherence to the policy of prohibition would put a great strain on the government of a country which could attract the industry. Nor is it clear that it would be in the best interests of the other countries that the industry should be established nowhere within the union.

The inflexibility of the allocation procedure and the direct bargaining between governments which it entails are among its undesirable features, and it would be helpful if an 'equalizing' mechanism could be found which did not possess these disadvantages. It is possible that an investment bank could be developed as a suitable instrument. It would, of course, be neither possible nor even desirable completely to isolate such a bank from political influences and requirements, but it could be sufficiently insulated from the immediate pressures to which a government department is subjected to be able to take a more detached view than would be possible for ministers bargaining over the location of a particular prospective industry. The functions of such a bank should be to increase the rate of industrial investment within the common-market area, and in this growth context to invest so as to bring forward the least-developed countries.

An investment bank could also serve as a channel through which foreign aid could be directed towards the purposes of economic integration. Both with fiscal transfers and with industrial allocation, the costs of regulation are imposed on members of the common market. Yet these are poor countries, and though they may be the gainers from the common market, they are unlikely to be more than a little less poor than the losers, and may not be even that. It is true that the purpose is to redistribute only part of their gains, but it remains a process of depriving countries which can ill afford to lose any benefits they might otherwise have received. The equalization necessary for the continuation of economic unions would be a suitable function for foreign aid to perform, and an investment bank might be a suitable instrument for the purpose.

If economic integration stimulates development, then aid which assists integration is efficient aid, serving the developmental purposes of aid. Unfortunately, aid can hinder rather than foster the process of integration. Aid which is given within the context of plans that are oriented purely nationally can both be wastefully used in the unnecessary multiplication of facilities and create an impediment to future integration. It is even worse where the aid is given for a plan which is inconsistent with those of neighbouring countries, as for example where a country plans to find a market in a neighbouring country which itself is planning for self-sufficiency. The politics of aid could lead to the establishment of industries within an economic union which conformed neither to the criterion of efficient location nor to that of a desirable intra-union balance of industry. Aid tied to the products of the donor country would make difficulties for an economic union if the products acquired from the donor would otherwise have been supplied from within the union. If the aid were not tied to specific goods the recipient would probably obtain from the donor products, particularly capital goods, which were not available from a partner state. The difficulty is likely to be more serious in the case of commodity aid and barter deals. These arrangements might well include the supply of consumer goods which are also produced within the economic union. The commitment to favour intra-union trade implicit in the existence of the tariff preference would be violated if goods were obtained from abroad as aid which would not have been bought if they had been offered under market conditions.

The problems of economic union which have been described are those which arise in an economic association between states which are politically separate. It might be argued that effective economic union can therefore be achieved only within the framework of a political association. It is true that the difficulties connected with supranational planning and with the revenue effects of customs unions are more or less automatically taken care of in a political association. But why should it be possible to sustain a political association if it were impossible to sustain the more limited measures of economic association? Why should it be easier to agree on many matters than on few? It could be the case, however, that despite the narrower range of issues in an economic union, the depth of agreement and common feeling required for anything but the most limited economic association are such that, if they were present, a political union would be as practicable as a purely economic union. Whether or not such a community of interest is necessary for an economic association is a question of great relevance to the future of economic co-operation between the countries of East Africa.

NOTES

[1] This chapter is based on Hazlewood, A., 'Problems of Integration among African States', in Hazlewood, A. (ed.), *African Integration and Disintegration* (London: Oxford University Press, 1967).

[2] The classic statement of the propositions of the theory is Viner, J., *The Customs Union Issue* (New York: Carnegie Endowment for International Peace, 1950). See also, for example, Meade, J. E., *The Theory of Customs Unions* (Amsterdam: North-Holland Publishing Co., 1955), and Lipsey, R. G., 'The Theory of Customs Unions: A General Survey', *Econ. J.*, Sept. 1960. For a critical examination of the theory see Cooper, C. A., and Massell, B. F., 'A New Look at Customs Union Theory', *Econ. J.*, Dec. 1965. Discussions of customs-union theory in relation to less-developed countries include Mikesell, R. F., 'The Theory of Common Markets as applied to Regional Arrangements among Developing Countries', in Harrod, R., and Hague, D., *International Trade Theory in a Developing World* (London: Macmillan, 1963), and Cooper, C. A., and Massell, B. F., 'Toward a General Theory of Customs Unions for Developing Countries', *J. Pol. Econ.*, Oct. 1965.

[3] The phrase is that of the Raisman Report: Colonial Office, *East Africa: Report of the Economic and Fiscal Commission*, Cmnd 1279 (London: HMSO, 1961).

3 *East African Integration: Origins and Development*

(A) THE COMMON MARKET

The customs union of the three territories (commonly referred to in East Africa as the common market) came into existence in stages over a considerable period of time.[1] Although there were subsequent changes in the arrangements for allocating customs revenue, the customs union of Kenya and Uganda was fully established by 1917, and from that date there was also a single customs administration for the two territories. Tanganyika was not brought fully into the union for another ten years, and it maintained a separate customs administration until the beginning of 1949.

Uganda, the East Africa Protectorate, and what was then German East Africa, originally each administered its own customs collections. Until the Uganda Railway provided a route into Uganda from Mombasa, the greater part of Uganda's imports came through German East Africa; goods for Uganda were regarded by the German administration as in transit and were not subject to duty. This was not the case at Mombasa, where duty was collected and retained by the East Africa Protectorate, whatever the ultimate destination of the goods. When they reached Uganda they were liable for import duty, but no further duty was collected if it could be shown that they had been imported through Mombasa. No problem arose until the opening of the Uganda Railway caused a transfer of Uganda's import traffic from German East African ports to Mombasa. As a result, Uganda's own collections declined, but she received no part of the revenue collected at Mombasa (*see* Table 3.1). In 1909 a first attempt was made to settle the problem by transferring revenue from Kenya. Initially the amount to be transferred was determined annually, but later it was agreed that Uganda should receive 25 per cent of the revenue collected at Mombasa.

By 1917, when the customs departments of Kenya and Uganda

were amalgamated, so large a part of Uganda's imports were being carried by the railway through Kenya that her own collection of customs revenue had become negligible. Free trade in local produce and in imported goods was provided for in the agreement establishing the common customs administration, so that the two territories had a common external tariff and internal free trade. The existing arrangement for the transfer of revenue to Uganda continued unamended until 1919, when the amount of the collection to be paid over was raised to 33 per cent. A radical change in the revenue allocation system came into effect at the beginning of 1923, the amount transferred then being based on estimates of the actual transfers of the dutiable goods to Uganda.

TABLE 3.1

Import duty revenue, Uganda

	£s	
	Direct collections	Transferred from Kenya
1908–9	3,285	..
1909–10	3,174	20,700
1916–17	224	68,826
1917–18	..	79,064

NOTE: .. = less than ½ unit.

Source: Kennedy, T. A., 'The East African Customs Union: Some Features of its History and Operation', *Makerere Journal*, 1959, p. 24.

Free trade between Kenya–Uganda and Tanganyika in local produce also began in 1923. However, imported goods were not made freely transferable throughout East Africa. Re-exports from Kenya–Uganda to Tanganyika, and *vice versa*, were treated in the same way as direct imports, and only in some cases was the duty originally paid refundable on re-export. This final barrier to the establishment of a full customs union was removed in 1927. At that time a system of Transfer Forms was also introduced from which the import duty revenue to be transferred from the collecting to the consuming territory was calculated, improving the accuracy of the allocation between Kenya and Uganda and extending it to Tanganyika. The arrangements completed in 1927 (they were extended to excise duties in the 1930s) remained the basis for the operation of the customs union. In summary, their main features were: an external tariff common to the three territories, but enacted separately in each territory; a single collection of import duty at the point of entry into East Africa and subsequent free movement of imported goods within East Africa; the allocation of customs revenue between the territories on the basis of 'derivation', that is, according to the territory of ultimate destination, the allocation being based on information from the Transfer Forms which were returned to the customs administration when goods were moved between the territories; free trade between the territories in products of East African origin; and from 1949 a common customs administration. In addition, there was free movement of capital and substantially free movement of labour. The economic unity of the area was supported, and transactions within the area fostered, by a common currency and the common administration of transport and communications and other 'infra-structure'.

From the beginning Uganda had a grievance against Kenya over customs matters. Although the major issue over revenue was removed with the reallocation introduced in 1909, dissatisfaction over details remained even after the principle of derivation was applied in 1923 and its administration improved in 1927. But more important were differences between the territories on the proper level and structure of the customs tariff.

Before the first world war the level of East African tariffs was restricted to 10 per cent by the Congo Basin Treaties. Uganda had originally imposed a tariff of 5 per cent, which was increased to 10 per cent in 1904, in an attempt to increase revenue. After the war the 10 per cent ceiling was removed, and in 1921 the basic rate of duty for Kenya–Uganda was raised to 20 per cent. Uganda's interest was in a relatively low tariff; her revenue at the time was more buoyant than that of Kenya and her import prices were already high because of heavy transport costs. She had little or no domestic activity which would benefit from protection. This difference in the interest of Uganda and Kenya was enhanced by further changes in the tariff. In 1922 new duties were introduced, some of which were highly protective of Kenya producers. The protection was mainly accorded to farmers and producers of processed agricultural products, and was provided particularly by the substitution of specific for *ad valorem* duties. Higher *ad valorem* rates for some products were also introduced, though these did not by any means always have a protective intention – for example, the 50 per cent on wines and 30 per cent on motor cars. The protective effect of the 1922[2] tariff should not be exaggerated, and the protective element in the tariff remained subordinate. Nevertheless, in 1922 the East African customs union consciously embarked on the protective policy it continued to pursue, and which according to persistent claims by Tanganyika and Uganda has been primarily protective of Kenyan interests. This attitude was well expressed in an official report of 1932, which recommended that 'Tanganyika should . . . cease to deplete her revenue and impoverish her citizens by protecting the products of her neighbours'.[3]

Some flexibility in the rigour of the common tariff was introduced in 1930 by the device of 'suspended' duties, which could be imposed by a territory on top of the basic duty, but which did not have to be applied by all. In addition, some rates of duty were reduced. However, the inequitable operation of the customs union remained a major issue between the territories, and no serious attempt was made to solve the problem until the end of the colonial period.

The practical effect of the protective tariffs on the mass of the population in the early days of the customs union cannot, in fact, have been great. The 1922 specific duties applied, for example, to butter and bacon, and it may be that the real objection was to the effect on European consumers resident in Uganda of the protection of European producers resident in Kenya. Later, as Africans moved more into the money economy, doubtless the burden fell on them. The statistical basis for any judgement of the effects of the tariff is slight. The existence of the customs union meant that there was no administrative machinery for the collection of statistics on trade between Kenya and Uganda until 1927, when the Transfer Form system was introduced. No data were available on the distribution of imported goods between the territories until 1923, when estimates began to be made as a basis for the allocation of revenue. The statistics for trade between Kenya–Uganda and Tanganyika are even more inadequate, for it is not possible precisely to separate trade for local consumption from that for subsequent re-export.[4] The figures in Table 3.2, however, give some idea of the

TABLE 3.2

Destination of exports

	Per cent of Total			
	1926	1938	1947	1961
Kenya to:				
East Africa	10	12	14	28
Elsewhere	90	88	86	72
Tanganyika to:				
East Africa	7	1	5	4
Elsewhere	93	99	95	96
Uganda to:				
East Africa	..	6	20	14
Elsewhere	100	94	80	86

Note: .. = less than ½ unit.

Source: *Annual Trade Reports.*

relevant magnitudes and suggest that inter-territorial trade was not of considerable importance, at least until after the second world war. But Table 3.2 in fact gives an exaggerated impression of the importance of inter-territorial exports to Uganda in the 1940s. Table 3.3 shows the contribution of cigarettes to Uganda's total inter-territorial exports. This item had become important after 1939, and by 1955 accounted for nearly three-quarters of Uganda's exports to the rest of East Africa. In the

TABLE 3.3

Uganda's inter-territorial exports

	£m.		
	1947	1955	1956
Cigarettes	1·6	5·7	2·8
Other items	1·0	2·2	1·7
Total	2·6	7·9	4·5

Source: *Annual Trade Reports.*

following year the manufacturer transferred to Kenya much of the production that had been carried on in Uganda. Inter-territorial exports which in 1955 had accounted for 10 per cent of Uganda's total exports had declined to 6 per cent in 1956. The pattern of inter-state trade, in which Uganda had been in surplus, assumed what came to be thought of as the standard pattern, in which Kenya was in surplus and the other territories in deficit.

TABLE 3.4

Balances in inter-territorial trade

	£m.	
	1955	1956
Kenya	..	+4·9
Tanganyika	−3·9	−4·2
Uganda	+3·9	−0·7

NOTE;: .. = less than ½ unit.

Source: *Annual Trade Reports.*

Before 1956 Kenya's relative strength in inter-territorial trade had been reflected, not in a consistently surplus position, but in a different and much more varied composition of her trade. Kenya's inter-territorial exports could not have been affected in the way Uganda's were affected in 1956 by the decision of a single enterprise, and manufactured goods of a more or less sophisticated nature were more important in Kenya's inter-territorial exports than in Tanganyika's. From 1956 a consistent and increasing surplus was added to these other characteristics, and it came to be felt more and more strongly in Tanganyika and Uganda that the customs union was designed for the benefit of Kenya.[5]

In the early 1950s Tanganyika and Uganda favoured the dismantling of the controls that had been used to stimulate local production during the war and early post-war years, whereas Kenya wished to retain them.

Economic co-operation continued, however, despite divergences of view. One example was the agreement that wheat should not be imported if supplies could be obtained from Kenya. The benefits of co-operation did not flow only in one direction. The wheat agreement was balanced by a corresponding agreement on the use of Uganda sugar, and Uganda obtained high protection for the Jinja textile factory when it was set up. Nevertheless, the arrangements were felt to be working so much to Kenya's advantage that it became increasingly difficult to obtain agreement on customs-duty refunds and protective tariffs, and a breach in the common tariff appeared when Tanganyika declined to increase the duty on wheat and enamelled hollow-ware. By the end of the 1950s it was widely appreciated that if the integration arrangements were to survive, their benefits would have to be spread more evenly.

(B) COMMON SERVICES

The first of the inter-territorial services was the Uganda Railway, which, despite its name, ran for most of its length through the territory of the East Africa Protectorate, later to be called Kenya. When the borders of Uganda were moved to the west, in 1902, the whole of the railway in fact lay in Kenya, traffic with Uganda being carried by steamer on Lake Victoria between Kisumu and Port Bell. The railway was not extended into Uganda, within its revised borders, until the late 1920s, and was opened for traffic to Kampala at the beginning of 1931. Finance for the original construction was provided by the United Kingdom, with a waiver of interest (repayment of capital was waived in 1939). The railway, which was renamed the Kenya and Uganda Railway, was administered under a General Manager as a department of the Kenya Government, and its revenues and expenditures were combined with the other finances of the government. In 1918 the Kenya Government imposed a surcharge on railway charges to assist its general revenue, to which Uganda objected. An attempt to accommodate the interests of both territories was made in 1925 with the establishment of a Railway Advisory Council, having equal representation from the two territories, the creation of the post of High Commissioner of Transport, to be occupied by the Governor of either Kenya or Uganda, and with an agreement to separate the finances of the railway from those of the Kenya Government. There were other difficulties between the territories, particularly over the structure of the railway tariff, which remained. Uganda argued that the structure of the charges, with high rates for imports, protected Kenya industry at the expense of Uganda consumers, and that there was an insufficient 'distance taper' in the tariff, thus favouring Kenya exports and discriminating against Uganda exports.[6]

Other common services established in the first decade of the century were a Court of Appeal, postal services, and Currency Commissioners, who issued local coin expressed in rupees against a reserve of sterling, although the main circulating medium consisted of imported Indian rupee coins.

The issue of currency for all three territories was put on a new basis with the establishment of the East African Currency Board at the end of 1919.[7] The Board completed the conversion of the existing coinage into East African shillings by 1925, and continued to provide the currency of the three territories, issuing shillings on an automatic sterling-exchange basis at the rate of E.A shs. 20/– to the pound sterling until the establishment of central banks in 1966. Until 1960 the head-quarters of the Board were in London, when they were transferred to Nairobi.

Developments in the common institutions during the 1920s included the extension of the jurisdiction of the East African Court of Appeal to Tanganyika, the establishment of an East African Office and a Trade Commissioner in London, and the amalgamation of the Posts and Telegraphs Departments of Kenya and Uganda. During the same decade, Mombasa harbour, which had been administered by the Kenya Government, was transferred to the railways administration, which was renamed Kenya–Uganda Railways and Harbours, and the East African Meteorological Department was set up. A permanent Secretariat for the East African Governors' Conference [see below, section (c)] was established in Nairobi in 1926, and the Statistical Adviser to the Kenya Government assumed the additional responsibility of providing statistical services to this Secretariat. Internal air services began to be provided in 1929.

In 1933 the Posts and Telegraphs Department of Kenya–Uganda was amalgamated with that of Tanganyika, providing an East African administration for both postal and telecommunications services, although the administration remained dependent on the governments for its finances until 1949, when it was established as a self-contained, self-financing organization. A central veterinary research organization for East Africa was established in 1939.

The second world war gave a considerable stimulus to inter-territorial organization, and various Boards and Councils came into existence. Some of these institutions were temporary, but others continued after the war, including the East African Industrial Research Organization. Income tax, which had been introduced in Kenya in 1937, was extended to the remainder of East Africa in 1940 under a common administration, and by agreement common rates were applied throughout East Africa.

After the second world war there was a development of research institutions on an East African basis. East African Airways Corporation was established in 1946, the Directorate of Civil Aviation was set up, and the separate administrations of Kenya–Uganda and Tanganyika for customs and railways were amalgamated to establish, respectively, the East African Customs and Excise Department and East African

Railways and Harbours. There were also the important changes in the government of the common institutions that are dealt with below [see section (c)].

When the developments following the end of the second world war were complete the common institutions for the three territories embraced the major transport and communications services (railways and harbours, posts and telecommunications, and airways); meteorological and civil aviation services; a range of research institutions which, in principle, were concerned with different, generally longer-term research than the corresponding territorial research institutions; revenue-collecting departments for customs, excise, and income tax; administrative services and economic services, including a statistical department; and some miscellaneous services such as the East African Literature Bureau. Higher education was also carried out in common for the three territories, and there was, of course, the common currency.

The economic unity of the area resulting from the common-market agreements and the common institutions stimulated and were reinforced by an 'East African attitude' in the private sector. The banks and many trading and manufacturing concerns treated East Africa as a unified area, and the territorial boundaries as commercially irrelevant. There were large seasonal movements of bank funds between the territories, and businesses operating throughout East Africa moved funds between their branches as their activities required. One consequence of this freedom of transactions was the growth of a belief in the other territories that Kenya, as the more developed centre, drained resources from them for her own use.

After this review of the very extensive range of matters on which by the end of the colonial period there was co-operation between the three governments, and of functions which were carried out on an East African basis, it is worth looking at the activities which might seem to have been appropriately carried out in common, but which in fact were not. They include the following:

(i) Airport and aviation ground services were the responsibility of the individual governments. Although the meteorological and flight-control services were on an East African basis, it was the responsibility of each government to build and maintain the airfields and to fix and collect aircraft landing fees and other charges for the use of the airports.

(ii) Road-transport licensing was a function of the individual governments (there was in fact no restrictive licensing control on road hauliers in Uganda), and road taxation was not co-ordinated between the three countries. Road development was also a matter for the individual governments. This entirely independent determination of the most important influences on the cost of road haulage, alongside the determination of railway policy and operations on an East African basis, made it difficult to achieve an economic distribution of traffic between road and rail, and hindered the development of transport on an East African basis.[8]

(iii) Although there was some attempt at the co-ordination of economic policies, and some was implicit in the fields of co-operation already mentioned, there was no common policy for economic development, let alone an East African development plan. The automatic character of the monetary system in effect prevented any of the governments from operating a monetary policy, and there was therefore no need for co-ordination in this field. A substantial measure of common policy was implicit in the agreed uniformity of the external tariff, in excise rates and income-tax rates. But the co-ordination which took place, particularly at budget time, was entirely on the revenue side. There was no co-ordination in the spending of the revenue – except that by the common services. At one time there were thoughts of an East African Development Plan. It was in this context that the industrial licensing system introduced in 1948 was originally devised. Its objective was to induce industries to set up in East Africa by regulating competition from rival firms; an Industrial Council was authorized to issue licences for the scheduled industries, having regard to both the applicant's resources and the general interest of East Africa. However, the council was not vested with authority to direct industries to suitable locations, as part of an overall plan, and the licensing system stagnated.

(C) THE GOVERNMENT OF INTEGRATION

No formal machinery for the government of the common arrangements that had developed existed before 1926. But for the whole of the 1920s the matter was under active public discussion in terms of proposals for the closer association, and particularly for a federation of the East African territories, and possibly of those further to the south. The pressures exerted in Britain and on the spot were complex. Fundamentally, the issue was between those who favoured the settlers, particularly the settlers in Kenya, where they were far more numerous than elsewhere, and those who were concerned to protect African interests. The former tended to favour closer association of the territories on the assumption that this was a precondition of any relaxation of Colonial Office control and its transfer into settler hands. The latter feared that closer association would in fact lead to dilution of the influence of Whitehall, and to the settlers' achieving a dominating position, and so they opposed closer association and favoured the maintenance of Imperial control. At the time majority rule was hardly conceived as an issue.

Five main State Papers dealt with the East African question between 1924 and 1931.[9] In the first of those years the Ormsby-Gore Commission was appointed, which came to the conclusion that federation was undesirable for practical reasons of the expense, and because of strong opposition from Indians and Africans. The Commission approved of increased economic co-ordination and recommended the holding of conferences of territorial Governors to achieve it.

In 1927 another commission, the Hilton Young Commission, was set up to examine the question of 'federation or some other form of closer union for effective co-operation between the different governments in Central and East Africa'. The Hilton Young Commission favoured federation, but on conditions that would have tended to reduce settler influence on affairs and to increase Imperial control, particularly over the protection of African interests. The proposals were rejected by the settlers and by the Colonial Office, which, in an attempt to remove the question from the sphere of politics into that of economic administration, sent an official, Sir Samuel Wilson, to re-examine the recommendations on the spot. Wilson proposed that a High Commission should administer the various common services, that policy concerning African interests should remain a territorial matter, and that the settlers should be given an enhanced position in Kenya, with a majority over officials in the Legislative Council.

The Labour Government which came into office in 1929 rejected these proposals and produced its own, which included a High Commissioner who, acting as the instrument of the Colonial Secretary, would administer the common services and would oversee the activities of the territorial governments so as to prevent racial discrimination. This scheme, with its element of increased Whitehall control, neither satisfied the settlers nor stilled the fears of Africans, particularly in Tanganyika and Uganda, that any move towards closer association of the territories would strengthen settler influence.

The final essay in closer association at this time was the Report of a Joint Select Committee of both Houses of Parliament, to which the matter had been referred. The Committee reported in 1931 against a political association on grounds both of expense and of a lack of consensus among the population of East Africa, but recommended the intensified use of Governors' Conferences to secure the benefits of economic co-ordination. With this echo of the Ormsby-Gore Report the matter rested until after the second world war.

While the discussion of closer association was being carried on, a form of government for the common arrangements came into existence. The Ormsby-Gore Commission's proposal was implemented in 1926, when the first Governors' Conference was held in Nairobi. The Conference established a permanent secretariat and continued to meet about once a year under the chairmanship of the Governor of Kenya. At its meetings the Conference discussed issues of railway rating, the customs tariff, and other matters of inter-territorial concern. Perhaps its major contribution was made during the war when it was responsible for co-ordinating the war effort of the territories.

After the war the British Government brought forward proposals to overcome the weaknesses of the existing inter-territorial arrangements in East Africa. The Governors' Conference, a White Paper explained,[10] had no legal or constitutional basis; it functioned without public debate or discussion; it could obtain the enactment of common legislation only by presenting identical ordinances to the three territorial legislatures, which they could not amend without destroying the necessary uniformity, so that their debates on the issues were unreal. The solution proposed was a High Commission, consisting of the three Governors, an executive organization, and a Central Legislative Assembly. The Assembly would have powers over the common services, including the tax-collecting departments for income tax and customs and excise, and over such matters as commercial law, industrial licensing, road transport, and customs tariff rates (though not over the rates of income tax). The proposals would have established a quite strong central organization, and because of the central legislative power over customs rates would have provided for the first time a firm legal basis for the common market. The Government disavowed any intention of establishing a federation, however, because it recognized the absence of both the community of interest and the public support that a political association would require.

The proposals encountered strong opposition from Europeans in East Africa over the composition of the Legislative Assembly, which involved equal representation for Africans, Asians and Europeans. The scheme that was ultimately introduced[11] had abandoned 'parity' in the CLA and some other features of the original proposals, including the central enactment of customs tariff rates and road-transport licensing.

The scheme for financing the High Commission services was also different from the original proposal. It was originally intended that the departmental expenditures (though not those of the research services) should be financed by a deduction from customs and excise revenues before they were handed over to the territories. In the arrangements adopted the High Commission services (other than those which were self-financing or which were financed by grants from the United Kingdom or elsewhere) were made dependent on annual appropriations by the territories.

The railways and harbours and postal and telecommunications services came to be known as the 'self-contained' services, because they financed their running costs from their earnings, though they were heavily dependent on outside sources for investment funds. East African Airways, in this sense, was also a self-contained service, though it was organized as a public corporation and its constitutional position was different. The 'non-self-contained' services were dependent on outside finance, partly provided by the territories, but also on a large scale from the United Kingdom and some other sources, particularly for the research services. Although higher education was provided in common its constitutional position was different from that of the High Commission services, and the Currency Board was always separate and autonomous.

It was intended that the High Commission should be an East African authority, and not simply a conference of Governors representing individual territorial interests. An implication of this intended status of the High Commission was that it should operate on the advice of its own officials, not those of the territories. In practice, the High Commission never became an independent East African authority in this sense. This was partly because of the circumscribed role allowed it in the scheme adopted, as compared with the original proposals, and partly because matters continued to be viewed primarily from a territorial standpoint. This unwillingness to put aside territorial interests and to view matters from an East African standpoint remained a central problem in the government of the common arrangements through all their subsequent changes. It may be wondered if it is realistic to expect success from arrangements which, if they are to work, require a submergence of territorial interests. Rather, the arrangements should be designed to work as a result of each territory pursuing its own interest; but it is easier to state the principle than to apply it.

Under the High Commission the services were administered by an Administrator and six other officers concerned with particular fields of responsibility – a Commissioner for Transport, a Postmaster General, a Financial Secretary, for example – who were in effect the ministers for the common services, though they were all 'officials', in the sense that they were not elected. They were members of the Legislative Assembly, which also included six territorial officials appointed by the Governors, together with twenty unofficial members; but eleven of these were also appointed by the Governors, and only nine elected by the territorial legislatures. This 'colonial' type of constitution closely resembled those of the territories at the time that it was introduced, but with constitutional progress in the territories the High Commission arrangements, with their entirely official executive, became increasingly anomalous. They were obviously inappropriate to a situation in which one or more of the territories had achieved independence.

NOTES

[1] Kennedy, T. A., 'The East African Customs Union: Some Features of its History and Operation', *Makerere Journal*, No. 3, 1959, summarizes and analyses the early history of the customs arrangements.

[2] Kennedy, op. cit., dates the tariff innovation as 1924, but this is a misprint.

[3] Colonial Office, *Report by Sir Sydney Armitage-Smith, K.B.E., C.B. on a Financial Mission to Tanganyika*, Cmd 4182 (London: HMSO, 1932) p. 25.

[4] For an examination of the early external trade statistics see Hazlewood, A., 'Statistics of Kenya and Uganda Imports, 1923–1948', and 'Consistent Trade Statistics of Kenya, Uganda and Tanganyika for 1950 and Earlier Years', East Africa Statistical Dept., *Econ. Statist. R.*, March and Dec. 1973.

[5] See Elkan, W. and Nulty, L., 'The Economic Links between Kenya, Uganda and Tanganyika' in Smith, A., and Low, D. A. (eds) *History of East Africa* Vol. III (Oxford: Clarendon Press, 1975), for a well-informed account of the situation in the 1950s. See also Ndegwa, P., *The Common Market and Development in East Africa* (Nairobi: East African Publishing House, 1965 and 1968), particularly for a detailed examination of trade between the middle 1950s and the middle 1960s.

[6] The history of the railways in East Africa is explained at length in Hill, M. F., *Permanent Way* (Nairobi: E.A.R. & H., vol. 1, 1949, vol. 2, 1957), and more concisely in Lord Hailey, *An African Survey* (London: Oxford University Press, rev. edn 1956) pp. 1556–61. See Colonial Office, *Report by Mr Roger Gibb on Railway Rates and Finance in Kenya, Uganda, and Tanganyika Territory*, Cmd 4235 (London: HMSO, 1933), which suggested that 'at the back of this [railway rates] policy lies half concealed the policy of subsidizing the Europeans at the expense of the natives'.

[7] Newlyn, W. T., and Rowan, D. C., *Money and Banking in British Colonial Africa* (Oxford: Clarendon Press, 1954) summarizes the history of the Currency Board and analyses the operations of the monetary system. See also Hazlewood, A., 'The Economics of Colonial Monetary Arrangements', *Economic and Social Studies*, Dec. 1954.

[8] See Hazlewood, A., *Rail and Road in East Africa* (Oxford: Blackwell, 1964), and 'The Co-ordination of Transport Policy', in Leys, C., and Robson, P., *Federation in East Africa* (Nairobi: Oxford University Press, 1965).

[9] Colonial Office, *East Africa: Report of the East Africa Commission* (W. G. Ormsby-Gore, Chairman), Cmd 2387 (London: HMSO, 1925); Colonial Office, *Report of the Commission on Closer Union of the Dependencies in Eastern and Central Africa* (Sir E. Hilton Young, Chairman), Cmd 3234 (London: HMSO, 1929); Colonial Office, *Report of Sir Samuel Wilson on his Visit to East Africa*, 1929, Cmd 3378 (London: HMSO, 1929); *Statement of the Conclusions of H.M.G. in the United Kingdom as regards Closer Union in East Africa*, Cmd 3574 (London: HMSO, 1930); House of Commons, *Joint Select Committee on Closer Union in East Africa Report and Minutes of Evidence*, H. C. 156 (London: HMSO, 1931, 3 vols). Rothchild, D., *Politics of Integration: An East African Documentary* (Nairobi: East African Publishing House, 1968) reproduces extracts from these and other basic documents in the history of East African integration and provides a useful guide to the literature.

[10] Colonial Office, *Inter-Territorial Organization in East Africa*, Col. 191 (London: HMSO, 1945).

[11] Colonial Office, *Inter-Territorial Organization in East Africa, Revised Proposals*, Col. 210 (London: HMSO, 1947).

4 *The Independence Settlement*

(A) THE RAISMAN REPORT

The previous chapter described the growth of the inter-territorial arrangements in East Africa and referred to the objections that, with varying degrees of intensity, were expressed from the beginning in Tanganyika and Uganda, where it was believed that the arrangements worked consistently to the advantage of Kenya and served to increase Kenya's influence over matters of common interest, and possibly over the territorial concerns of Tanganyika and Uganda. The strength of feeling arose not only from the belief that the economic benefits of the common arrangements accrued to Kenya, at the expense of the other territories, but also from a fear of the political influence of a settler-dominated Kenya. There had, after all, been the experience of Central Africa, where what were then Northern Rhodesia and Nyasaland had been forced into a federation with settler-dominated Southern Rhodesia.[1] There was a real fear, particularly in Uganda, that something similar might take place in East Africa. By 1960 the grounds for this particular fear had been removed, for it was clear that Tanganyika and Uganda were to become independent, and that independence with an African-majority government was bound to follow in Kenya. But by then the economic grounds for objections to the common arrangements had become stronger. The export boom of the mid-1950s had come to an end and the supposed costs of the common market – the protection of Kenyan manufacturing and the fiscal strait-jacket of common rates of import and excise duty and income tax – assumed increased importance.

At the end of the colonial period an attempt was made to put the common arrangements on a satisfactory basis for the future. A commission was appointed under Sir Jeremy Raisman to examine the arrangements, to consider their advantages and disadvantages, and in particular whether they were fair to the individual territories, and to make recommendations for any necessary adjustments, additions, or modifications to them.

The Raisman Report[2] contains the most careful analysis available in an official document of the operation of the common market. The Commission showed themselves to be well aware of the possible disadvantages of the common market for Tanganyika and Uganda arising from the position of Kenya as the more developed territory, but they also noted the beneficial 'spill-over effects' on the other territories of the development of Kenya. Perhaps they did not sufficiently consider whether the attractiveness of Kenya for investors would deprive the other territories of capital and limit their ability to respond to the spill-over of demand. However, they took the view that Tanganyika and Uganda were not simply primary producers selling in world markets, unable to benefit from the customs union, and would in fact gain rather than lose in real income from the growth of protected industry in Kenya. The Commission concluded that the common market benefited East Africa as a whole, that its working could be validly criticized for producing an unequal distribution of the benefits, rather than for imposing losses on any member, and that no territory would be likely to gain from withdrawing. They also pointed out, in an important passage of their report,[3] that:

> As development tends to bring increased specialisation and increased reliance upon activities in which the minimum efficient scale of operations is large, the contributions which the Common Market arrangements can make to economic growth are likely to be greater in the future than in the past.

The Commission argued that some of the criticisms of the common market were properly criticisms of the effect of various impediments to the free operation of the market, arising mainly from statutory marketing, which led to clashes of interest between the territories. They proposed measures for improved economic co-ordination between the territories as a way to minimize such clashes of interest.

The Raisman Commission also recognized the difficulties for a territory arising from the fiscal constraint imposed by the inability to vary the main tax-rates unilaterally, and they proposed that these difficulties should be dealt with by a device that would also compensate for the inequalities of development within the common market: a fiscal redistribution. Their proposals for a Distributable Pool of revenue are examined later in this chapter. The same device was to settle a major problem of the common services, the dependence on annual subventions from the territories, by providing the services with an independent source of revenue.

The Raisman Report did not make detailed proposals on constitutional forms. The Commission remarked on the gap that had developed between the constitutional position of the High Commission and of the territories. They also noted the need for a central body for the supervision and management of the common services, and central machinery for co-ordinating and harmonizing territorial policies affecting the common market. At least some of these needs were taken into account later in 1961, when new arrangements were introduced which embodied the main proposals of the Raisman Commission.

(B) THE EAST AFRICAN COMMON SERVICES ORGANIZATION

At discussions held in June 1961 between delegations from the United Kingdom, the three East African territories, and the High Commission administration, it was agreed that it would be in the interest of all the territories that the common services should continue to be provided on an East African basis. It was further agreed that the administration of the services under the High Commission should be brought to an end upon the achievement of independence by Tanganyika, in December 1961. The administration of the services should be undertaken by a new organization, the East African Common Services Organization, the responsibility for the policy of which should rest with the East African Common Services Authority consisting of the principal elected ministers of the three territorial governments (and later, by a natural extension, the three Heads of State).[4]

The establishment of the new organization was the inter-territorial counterpart of the independence of the East African countries, and its policies were in the hands of the ministers of the three governments. Under the Authority the Organization was controlled by 'triumvirates' of ministers. There were four triumvirates, with responsibility respectively for Communications, Finance, Commercial and Industrial Co-ordination, and Social and Research Services. Later, a fifth triumvirate concerned with labour questions was created. The triumvirates consisted of the ministers responsible for the relevant matters in the territorial governments, the Finance Ministers composing the Finance triumvirate, the Ministers for Communications the Communications triumvirate, and so on. The triumvirates met separately to deal with their particular responsibilities, and also together so as to secure co-ordination of EACSO activities. To reach a decision on a matter of policy unanimity was required of a triumvirate, and if agreement proved impossible an issue could be referred to the Authority for a decision.

The administration of the common services was in the hands of a Secretary-General. The other senior executive officers were the General Manager of the Railways and Harbours Administration, the Postmaster General, the Legal Secretary, the Financial Secretary, and the Auditor-General. An executive officer was associated with each of the triumvirates and was responsible for giving effect to its decisions.

Legislation on the matters for which the Organization was responsible was passed by the Central Legislative Assembly consisting of the twelve (later fifteen) members of the triumvirates, the Secretary-General and the Legal Secretary of EACSO, and nine members from each territory elected by the territorial legislature. The Assembly had legislative powers over the common services administered by the Organization, both self-contained and non-self-contained, including the customs and excise and income-tax administrations, but it had no powers over the rates of taxation, which were a matter for the territorial legislatures. It could also legislate on some matters which, strictly speaking, were not services of the Organization, and for which EACSO had no administrative responsibility, in particular the university institutions of East Africa, the East African Court of Appeal, and East African Airways. Legislation passed by the CLA was forwarded for the assent of the Authority. Territorial legislation provided for Acts of the Assembly to have the force of law in each of the territories.

The financial arrangements of the non-self-contained services had already been amended before EACSO came into formal existence. From 1 July 1961, the beginning of the 1961–2 financial year, the reliance of the services on annual appropriations by the territorial legislatures was abandoned, and they were financed from a General Fund. The creation of such an independent source of revenue for the services as recommended by the Raisman Commission was associated with the fiscal redistribution proposals of the Commission, which are dealt with in the final section of this chapter.

Some of the stresses and strains in the relationships between the three members of EACSO which developed after 1961, and which are discussed in Chapter 6, can be traced to weaknesses inherent in the structure of the Common Services Organization. Other weaknesses in the working of the Organization cannot, perhaps, be blamed on its structure, but none the less made for difficulties in the relations between the member states.[5]

The placing of the control of the Organization, under the Authority, in the hands of the triumvirates of territorial ministers led to EACSO affairs taking second place to national affairs. The ministers were primarily concerned with their national ministries, and an unwillingness or inability to devote enough time to EACSO matters led to delays, infrequent meetings of the triumvirates, and difficulties for the officials of the Organization in obtaining directives and decisions. The ministers found it difficult to identify themselves as East African ministers, rather than territorial ministers, in dealing with EACSO affairs. Their association with EACSO officials was far less close and frequent than with national civil servants, on whom they mainly relied for advice on EACSO as well as on national matters (a point made by the Raisman Commission about the previous arrangements). Ministers played the role of delegates mandated by their governments in inter-territorial negotiations rather than that of leaders of a supranational authority.

The Legislative Assembly, though it had the advantage over the CLA under the High Commission in having a smaller representation of officials of the administration, still lacked political significance. It legislated formally on matters about which decisions had already been taken by the Authority, so that its powers and responsibilities were much less than those of the territorial legislatures. Although there was often lively and critical debate, too often the concern of members was with the territorial advantages rather than those of East Africa as a whole.

The power of initiative permitted EACSO officials by the member countries was narrow. However competent and enthusiastic the members of the administration might be, their limited scope for exercising initiative ensured that a strong bureaucracy committed to forwarding the process of co-operation between the countries could not develop.

The staffing of the Organization was, in fact, a cause of contention between the countries. There were complaints that an inordinate proportion of EACSO officials were Kenyans. One reason was that the headquarters of the Organization were in Kenya, as were most of the other departments and institutions. It was said to be easier to recruit Kenyans for this reason, and also because the supply of suitable candidates for the appointments at that time was much greater from Kenya than from the other two countries. No thought was given, it appears, to the possibility of national quotas in appointments, and from the point of view of efficiency it may well have been correct not to do so.

More important than the predominance of Kenyans in the EACSO administration as a point of contention between the countries, was the continued concentration in Kenya of so much of the apparatus of the inter-territorial arrangements. The opportunity offered by the creation of the new Organization to modify this concentration in Kenya was not taken. The headquarters of all the self-contained services, including the airways, and the headquarters of the Organization itself, were in Nairobi. The income-tax and customs headquarters were in Kenya, as also were those of the Directorate of Civil Aviation, the Meteorological Department, and other services. The research institutions were more evenly distributed between the three members, but this did little in terms of the employment given by the Organization and its expenditures to reduce the dominance of Kenya. The material benefits of the location of so much of the expenditures of the Organization in Kenya was a matter which became of serious concern. The view that the location of its headquarters in Nairobi gave the Organization a 'Kenya' outlook was important for relations between the member countries. Whatever the truth of the matter, it was believed that their location in Nairobi, their ready access to Kenya Government officials, and the large number of them who were Kenyans, when they were not expatriates, gave the officials of EACSO a Kenyan bias which the other members thought inimical to their interests.

It was also believed that there was a bias in favour of Kenya in the revenue-collection system. The calculation of the customs revenue due to Uganda and Tanzania on imported goods transferred from Kenya was claimed to work to their disadvantage. The location in Kenya of the head offices of companies operating throughout East Africa was said to give Kenya an undue share of the income-tax revenue from such companies. Complaints of this kind were not totally silenced by the existence of the system of fiscal redistribution which was introduced in 1961.

(C) FISCAL REDISTRIBUTION

The most important of the proposals of the Raisman Commission were those concerning finance. It has already been pointed out that the aim of the proposal was to provide an independent source of finance for the common services and to secure a fiscal redistribution between the territories. These purposes were to be achieved through the creation of a Distributable Pool.

Some services, the Commission believed, 'because of various uncertainties surrounding them', should continue to be financed by specific annual appropriations from the territorial revenues; the costs of the revenue-collecting departments should be a first charge on the revenue collected; and the remainder of the non-self-contained services, it was proposed, should be financed from an independent source of revenue with which the High Commission should be provided. The Raisman Report argued that:

> Possession by the High Commission of an independent revenue would assist these services in their activities by providing them with a greater certainty of funds and it would also promote a more efficient use of funds between services by enabling the High Commission to function as a single authority, able – with the advice of its various boards, councils and committees – to administer its services from the point of view of the interests of the whole of East Africa rather than as an agency of territorial Governments.[6]

This independent source of revenue should come from the Distributable Pool. In each year one-half of the receipts of the Pool, the report recommended, should be distributed to the High Commission for financing its services.

The main purpose, however, in establishing the Distributable Pool was to achieve some inter-territorial redistribution of revenue. In making the proposal for the revenue Pool the Commission stated:

> The future political relationship between the Territories cannot be predicted or prejudged. We think, however, that the Common Market is of such importance to their economic future, and the danger to it from internal strains so great, that some inter-territorial redistribution of income, offsetting in some degree the inequalities in the benefits derived, is urgently called for in order that the Market may be preserved.[7]

The proposal, which was first put into effect for the 1961–2 financial year, was that 6 per cent of the customs and excise collections and 40 per cent of the yield of 'income tax charged to companies on profits arising from manufacturing and finance' should be paid into a Distributable Pool. One-half the annual receipts of the Pool was to go, as was explained above, to finance the High Commission; the remaining half was to be distributed equally between the three territories. The direct redistributive effect is clear. Each territory was to receive the same amount, but they would contribute to the Pool in proportion to the revenue collected from them. A change in the relative revenue yields in the territories would be automatically reflected in the magnitudes of the redistribution. There would be also an indirect redistribution achieved by the Pool, the Report argued, because of the new method of financing the High Commission services.

In justifying the magnitude of the redistribution they expected to achieve through their proposals, the Commission reiterated the point that their primary object was 'to offset, by fiscal means, the inequalities in the distribution of benefits from the Common Market'. It is to be noted that the proposed fiscal transfers were related to the distribution of all the benefits of the common market, not merely to losses of revenue by any members, but they did not take any account of the distribution of the net benefits of the common services. The Commission argued that it was 'impracticable to make any precise estimates of the amount of fiscal adjustment which is called for'. The adjustment required was 'a matter for the exercise of judgment rather than of minute statistical calculation', but this did not mean, they hastened to add, 'that our proposals are arbitrary'.[8]

Arbitrary or not, the Commission provided no details of the basis for the exercise of their judgement, merely stating that:

> Our decision as to the appropriate order of magnitude for the fiscal adjustment to be achieved through the Pool has been made after careful assessment of the evidence regarding effects on the Territories of the present Common Market arrangements, and after allowing for our recommendations for improved economic co-ordination.[9]

Perhaps the Commission's view of the magnitude of the inequalities requiring to be compensated may be deduced from the example they give of the redistributive effect of their proposals. It will be seen from Table 4.1, which is derived from the Raisman Report, that the Commission concluded that a transfer from Kenya to Tanganyika of £310,000 and to Uganda of £245,000, plus £120,000 additional resources of the High Commission, with the indirect redistribution through the finances of the High Commission Services, was adequate compensation.

It must, of course, be agreed that an estimate of the necessary redistribution is a matter of judgement. In forming their judgement the

TABLE 4.1

Redistributive effect of Distributable Pool: Raisman Report example

(a) Receipts (net of collection cost) of DP from:

	£'000
Kenya	1,735
Tanganyika	775
Uganda	700
Total receipts of DP	3,210

(b) Distribution of distributable pool:

	£'000
½ to High Commission	1,605
1/6 to Kenya	535
1/6 to Tanganyika	535
1/6 to Uganda	535
Total payments from DP	3,210

(c) Redistribution

	£'000		
	Kenya	Tanganyika	Uganda
(*a*) Payments into DP for redistribution	867	387	350
(*b*) Receipts from DP	535	535	535
(*c*) Fiscal redistribution	−332	+148	+185
Payments for common services:			
(*d*) 'Present' system	525	550	410
(*e*) 'Proposed' by Raisman	867	387	350
(*f*) Gain/loss from 'proposed' system	−342	+163	+60
(*g*) Total redistribution ((*c*) + (*f*))	−675	+310	+245

NOTES:

1. The total payments from each territory into the DP can be thought of as being 50 per cent for redistribution to the territories and 50 per cent for the finance of the common services because the total receipts of the Pool are divided in this way.
2. The net redistribution from the territories taken together is −120 (i.e. −675 + 310 + 245), which is the increase in contribution to the High Commission under the Raisman proposal.
3. Rows and columns do not always add because of rounding.

Source: Colonial Office, *East Africa: Report of the Economic and Fiscal Commission*, Cmnd 1279 (London: HMSO, 1961) pp. 82–3.

TABLE 4.2

Revenue redistribution through the Distributable Pool

	£'000				
	1961–2	1962–3	1963–4	1964–5	1965–6
(a) *Payments into DPF from*					
Kenya	1,731	2,092	2,551	2,499	2,935
Tanganyika	791	1,028	1,164	1,329	1,380
Uganda	759	830	1,159	1,590	1,445
Total receipts of DPF	3,281	3,950	4,874	5,418	5,760
(b) *Distribution of DPF*					
1/2 to general Fund	1,640	1,975	2,438	2,709	2,880
1/6 to Kenya	547	658	812	903	960
1/6 to Tanganyika	547	658	812	903	960
1/6 to Uganda	547	658	812	903	960
Total payments from DPF	3,281	3,950	4,874	5,418	5,760
(c) *Distribution of receipts in absence of DPF*					
Assumption A (50% of each territory's payments paid to Common Services, 50% returned to territory)					
Receipts by:					
Kenya	865	1,046	1,275	1,249	1,467
Tanganyika	395	514	582	665	690
Uganda	379	415	579	795	723
Common Services	1,640	1,975	2,438	2,709	2,880
Total receipts	3,281	3,950	4,874	5,418	5,760
Assumption B (equal payments to Common Services; remainder of payment returned to territory)					
Receipts by:					
Kenya	1,184	1,434	1,739	1,596	1,975
Tanganyika	244	370	352	426	420
Uganda	212	173	347	687	485
Common Services	1,640	1,977	2,436	2,709	2,880
Total receipts	3,281	3,950	4,874	5,418	5,760
(d) *Territorial redistribution through Distributable Pool*					
Assumption A					
Kenya	−318	−388	−463	−346	−508
Tanganyika	+152	+144	+230	+238	+270
Uganda	+168	+243	+233	+108	+237
Assumption B					
Kenya	−637	−776	−927	−693	−1,015
Tanganyika	+303	+288	+460	+477	+540
Uganda	+335	+485	+465	+216	+475

NOTE: The payment into the Distributable Pool from each country is the sum of 6 per cent of customs and excise duty collected from that country and 40 per cent

Commission made a good deal of use of the available statistics. The conclusions they drew from their examination of the statistics has not gone unchallenged. But perhaps the most relevant comment is that:

> it is wiser to recognize that this sort of calculation [i.e. of rates of growth] cannot be carried out in East Africa at the present time with present data, with any pretence at reliability. Until this can be done, discussion of the real growth of any territory's economy, either in isolation or in relation to its neighbours', can only be in the most general terms and even then only the most tentative conclusions can be drawn.[10]

No attempt is made in this chapter at an independent assessment of what was required in the way of redistribution. It follows, however, from the argument of Chapter 5, below, that the case for redistribution as *compensation* was not strong, because the disequalizing effects of the common market have commonly been exaggerated, and there is reason to be sceptical of a claim that any country had been made worse off through its operation. But there are other and stronger arguments for redistribution. A case for redistribution follows from the contention that measures to diminish the differences between the three countries in the level of development were in themselves desirable, as well as necessary if the common market were to hold together.

Whatever view is taken of the reasons for redistribution, it cannot be thought that the direct redistribution the Commission expected to achieve was more than modest. This conclusion is not surprising, given

---

of the income tax on company profits from manufacture and finance *minus* the DPF share of the costs of collection divided between the countries in proportion to the costs of collection debited directly to the countries. The collection of income tax in the UK is allocated between the countries in proportion to the tax collected in each.

The allocation of the DPF receipts in the absence of the DPF is made on the assumption that the same total amount would be paid into the General Fund for the finance of EACSO services (i.e. an amount equal to 50 per cent of the payments into the DPF), but the rest would remain with or be returned to the countries of origin. A further assumption must be made about how, in the absence of the DPF, the payments into the General Fund would be divided between the countries. Under assumption 'A' the common services are financed essentially in the same way as under the Raisman arrangements, each country paying 50 per cent of the amount it pays into the DPF into the General Fund. Under assumption 'B' the three countries contribute equally to the General Fund. This assumption is a rough approximation to the position before the institution of the Raisman arrangements.

The measure of the inter-territorial redistribution through the Distributable Pool is arrived at as the difference (plus or minus) between the revenue received by each country from the Distributable Pool under the Raisman arrangement and the amount that would be received (under assumptions 'A' and 'B') if the Distributable Pool did not exist, a minus sign indicating that the territory loses and a plus sign that it gains from the operation of the Distributable Pool.

Source: EACSO, *Financial Statements* (annual).

the general tone of the Commission's discussion of the disequalizing effect of the common market, which gives the impression that they thought the other territories did not have much to worry about.

It is not a straightforward matter to calculate the fiscal redistribution that did take place through the Distributable Pool. The presentation in Table 4.1 of the Raisman Report's example of how the Pool would operate draws attention to the problem facing an attempt to estimate the redistribution, namely that some assumption must be made about how the common services would be financed in the absence of the Distributable Pool. It was easy enough for the Raisman Commission, for they merely had to compare the effect of their proposals with the then existing situation. But in order to estimate the redistribution achieved by the Raisman system in practice it is necessary to make a comparison with some assumed situation in which the Distributable Pool did not exist.

To limit the range of possibilities it has been assumed in the estimates of the redistribution presented in Table 4.2 that the same total finance would be available for the common services if it was provided other than through the Pool. Even given this limiting assumption, a wide range of possibilities exists with respect to the relative contributions made by each country to the total finance of the common services. The alternative assumptions that have been adopted for the estimates correspond to the 'Raisman' (Assumption A) and the 'pre-Raisman' (Assumption B) situations. In the one, the territories contribute to the finance of the common services in proportion to their revenues, while in the other they contribute equally.

The redistribution is measured by the change in the revenue of each government that would result from the abolition of the DP. Assumption 'A' envisages a situation in which the Pool is abolished but there is no change in the contribution of each territory to the finance of the common services. Assumption 'B' envisages a return to roughly the pre-Raisman situation. The estimated redistribution under assumption 'B', in the first year of the system, is broadly the same as that in the Raisman Report's illustrative exercise, and is roughly double that under assumption 'A'. As compared with the situation before the adoption of the Raisman proposals, including the system then in force for financing the common services, the redistribution achieved through the Distributable Pool is quite substantial by 1966, but if it is assumed that the abolition of the Pool would remove only the direct fiscal transfers the redistribution is reduced by half and is not large.

It is clear that there is no unique measure of the redistribution of revenue achieved through the Distributable Pool. The extent of redistribution varies with the assumption made about how the General Fund services of EACSO would have been financed in the absence of the Distributable Pool. It would not, in fact, have been realistic at the time when the system was adopted to assume that the alternative was the continuation of the arrangements existing in 1960. Indeed, the Raisman Commission, in illustrating the likely effect of their proposals, pointed out that the basis of allocating the costs of some common services in force at the time was 'actively disputed and would probably not be maintained in 1961/2 even if our recommendations did not supervene'. As it turned out, when the Distributable Pool was abandoned, the common services continued to be financed broadly as under the Raisman arrangements, in other words, as under Assumption 'A' of Table 4.2 (*see* Chapter 7).

NOTES

[1] See Rotberg, R. I., 'The Federation Movement in British East and Central Africa, 1889–1953', *J. of Commonwealth Political Studies*', May 1964, and Hazlewood, A., 'The Economics of Federation and Dissolution in Central Africa', in Hazlewood, A. (ed.), *African Integration and Disintegration* (London: Oxford University Press, 1967).

[2] Colonial Office, *East Africa: Report of the Economic and Fiscal Commission*, Cmnd 1279 (London: HMSO, 1961).

[3] Cmnd 1279, para. 191.

[4] See Colonial Office, *The Future of East Africa High Commission Services. Report of the London Discussions, June, 1961*, Cmnd 1433 (London: HMSO, 1961).

[5] See Banfield, J., 'The Structure and Administration of the East African Common Services Organization'; Nye, J. S., 'The Extent and Viability of East African Co-operation', in Leys, C., and Robson, P., *Federation in East Africa* (Nairobi: Oxford University Press, 1965); Proctor, J. H., and Krishna, K. G. V., 'The East African Common Services Organization: An Assessment', *S. Atlantic Q.*, Autumn 1965; and Segal, A., *East Africa: Strategy for Economic Co-operation* (Nairobi: East African Institute of Social and Cultural Affairs, 1965).

[6] Cmnd 1279, para. 205.

[7] Cmnd 1279, para. 203.

[8] Cmnd 1279, para. 210.

[9] ibid.

[10] Tyrrell, J., 'A Note on Mr Haddon-Cave's Measurements of Real Growth of the East African Territories, 1954–1960', *East Afr. Econ. R.*, Dec. 1961.

5 The Assessment of Benefits and Costs

The evident dissatisfaction with the equity of the common arrangements, which continued despite the fiscal redistribution, led to attempts
at an objective assessment of the benefits and of their distribution. The
first systematic essay at such an assessment had in fact already been
undertaken, by the Raisman Commission.[1]

One range of issues concerns the extent to which East Africa constituted a unified market, and the extent to which the existence of a
unified market was the result of the customs union. The absence of
tariffs is not a sufficient condition for the existence of a unified market –
transport costs between different parts of the area may be prohibitive.
The tariff preference created by the customs union may not be the
major determinant of the level of intra-union trade. The Raisman
Commission measured the size of the East African market compared
with that of any individual territory by aggregating the national incomes
of the three territories. This is a crude measure, even when supported
by their judgement that transport facilities and other infra-structure
did enable the East African market to function as a unified market.[2]

To measure the increased size of the East African market as compared
with that of an individual territory by the aggregate national income
takes no account, in the first place, of the area over which that income
is 'spread'. One way to do so is to calculate what has been called the
'purchasing power density' (PPD) of a country or region by expressing
national income per unit of land area.[3] But PPD is an inadequate
indication of the size of the market in a country within whose borders
there are wide differences in population and income density. In many
countries, much of the population and economic activity is concentrated in a relatively small part of the total area, and then the GDP per
square mile is not a very good indicator of the size of the market. A
better indication is provided by an index derived from a comparison of

the distribution of population and of land area between administrative units.[4] If population were evenly distributed over the surface area of the country or region, each administrative unit would contain the same proportion of population as of land area, and the index would have a value of zero. If the whole population were concentrated in one, small, administrative unit the value of the index would approach 100. The index can be improved as a measure of the location of the market by 'weighting' the population with a measure of income (*see* Table 5.1).

TABLE 5.1

Index of concentration of (unweighted) population

Kenya	65·4
Tanzania	38·6
Uganda	32·4
East Africa	50·4

Index of concentration of (income-weighted) population

Kenya	71·6
Tanzania	41·3
Uganda	34·9
East Africa	55·3

Source: Hazlewood, A., 'An Approach to the Analysis of the Spatial Distribution of the Market in East Africa', *Bulletin of the Oxford University Institute of Economics and Statistics*, November 1969.

The values of the unweighted index indicate a rather high degree of concentration, particularly in Kenya. Using the income-weighted population data an even higher degree of concentration is indicated. An intuitive way of expressing the meaning of these values is that the concentration of (unweighted) population was such that, in effect, 50 per cent of the land area of East Africa was unpopulated. For Kenya the corresponding figure is 65 per cent, for Tanzania 39 per cent, and for Uganda 32 per cent.

But these indices are also inadequate, for the same value could arise from widely different distributions of population. Population could be concentrated in a particular part of the country, or it could be located in a number of widely dispersed clusters, and the index would give the same value, although the size of the market facing a producer in some particular place would be very different in these two situations. What is missing is a measure of the location of population and economic activity in relation to the main transport facilities. This is provided by the figures in Table 5.2.

The figures show a rather high degree of concentration of the market in East Africa. They suggest that the extent to which East Africa was effective as a unified market was the consequence not only of the absence of tariffs and quantitative restrictions on inter-state trade, and the existence of the common external tariff, but also of the development of transport facilities and the location of population and economic activity in relation to them.[5] There were also institutional characteristics which helped the economic unity of the area. Commercial law and practice in the three countries was broadly similar, and there were strong commercial and financial links between them. It has already been remarked that many business firms treated East Africa as a unit for their operations.

TABLE 5.2

Percentage of population located near main transport routes

Kenya	71
Tanzania	45
Uganda	63
East Africa	59

Percentage of income-weighted population located near main transport routes

Kenya	81
Tanzania	52
Uganda	69
East Africa	68

Source: Hazlewood, A., op. cit.

The statistical analysis behind the figures in Tables 5.1 and 5.2 may be extended to throw light on the determinants of the importance of Nairobi in the economy of East Africa. Some historical reasons for Nairobi's importance have been mentioned in Chapter 1. In addition, Nairobi owed its importance to its location in relation to the distribution of the East African market. Of course, the causation was not one-way. Nairobi was favourably located in relation to the market partly because the market had grown up around Nairobi. There was a cumulative process at work, the outcome being that Nairobi was better located to serve the whole East African market than any other centre of production in East Africa. Not only did Nairobi have good transport links with the main areas of Kenya and Uganda, but northern Tanzania, including the relatively wealthy area around Moshi and Arusha, had closer links with Kenya than it had with the remainder of Tanzania. The statistical analysis indicates that Nairobi had a significant advantage in terms of 'market potential' over other production centres, and particularly over Dar es Salaam, and that Nairobi's advantage over Kampala derived from its location in relation to the high-income, non-African population, rather than from the spatial location of population as a whole in relation to Nairobi. The analysis leads to the further conclusion that more than half the potential market for producers in Nairobi and Mombasa derived from Kenya, the remainder deriving more or less equally from Tanzania and Uganda. The Tanzania centres, Dar es Salaam and Arusha, each derived under one-third of their market potential from Tanzania but almost half of the total from Kenya. Similarly, roughly one-third of the market potential of Kampala derived from Uganda, and not far short of a half from Kenya. Looked at in this way, paradoxically, the existence of the common market seems of much greater importance for Tanzania and Uganda than for Kenya, in the sense that the potential East African market open to producers in Tanzania and Uganda depends much more on access to the Kenya market than the market open to producers in Kenya depends on access to the Tanzania and Uganda markets.

The existence of factors other than the absence of tariffs in determining the unity of the East African market is relevant to the assessment not only of the importance of the common market but also of the distribution of its benefits. The distinction between the importance to producers of the East African market and of the common market, that is the tariff preference, needs to be emphasized. The Raisman Report did not sufficiently emphasize the distinction. The tariff preference has obviously nothing to do with the sale of electricity from Uganda to Kenya, yet the Raisman Report refers to it as an example of inter-territorial trade in the course of a discussion in which 'common market' and 'East African market' are used interchangeably.[6] An analysis of the pattern of trade and tariffs in 1962 indicated that a substantial part of inter-territorial trade was independent of the tariff preference.[7] In the first place, some products traded inter-territorially were not subject to duty when imported from outside East Africa. Inter-territorial trade in these products obviously had nothing to do with the common market. Secondly, it is relevant to remember that the East African tariff had been essentially a 'revenue tariff', and although it obviously had a protective effect it is not surprising that local production was not entirely dependent on the protection afforded.

The East African market for some Kenyan products was assisted by a 'transport protection' within East Africa (goods produced in Nairobi have a transport advantage in Uganda and parts of Tanzania over goods imported at Mombasa), although in fact the protection afforded was small. More important was the fact that some goods internally traded had no effective competitors from abroad – liquid milk is an obvious example. Other products important in inter-territorial trade were competitive in price and quality (allowing for the establishment of brand loyalty) with imports, so that their market did not rely on the tariff preference. Beer was an important example of such a product. Cigarettes were in much the same position; and in addition a substantial proportion of local sales was of cheap brands which had no likely imported competitor. Other products which, although nominally protected, had an East African market which was probably little dependent on the tariff preference were those which found export markets outside East Africa. (A number of manufactures were exported, mostly to neighbouring countries.) It cannot be proved logically that inter-territorial trade in such products did not depend upon the tariff preference, but the fact that they were able to compete in third countries provides a strong presumption that this was so.

In Tables 5.3 and 5.4 the trade classified as independent of the tariff

TABLE 5.3

Inter-territorial exports, 1962

	£m.			
	Kenya	Uganda	Tanganyika	Total
Independent of preference	8·6	4·3	1·4	14·3
Dependent on preference	8·7	2·8	1·0	12·5
Total	17·3	7·1	2·4	26·8

Source: Hazlewood, A., 'The East African Common Market: Importance and Effects', *Bulletin of the Oxford University Institute of Economics and Statistics*, February 1966.

TABLE 5.4

Importance of Common Market: inter-territorial exports as per cent of money GDP

	Kenya	Uganda	Tanganyika
Total inter-territorial exports	10	7	2
Inter-territorial exports dependent on preference	5	3	1

Source: Hazlewood, A., op. cit.

preference is the sum of trade in those commodities which, it was argued above, did not require the tariff preference to find an East African market, including trade in products on which the nominal rate in the East African customs tariff was zero. It will be seen that in 1962 only about one-half of inter-territorial trade was dependent on the tariff preference. Massell also took the view that the common market was relatively unimportant in the early 1960s. He suggested that 'if the common market broke up, in the short run the result would be only a one or two per cent decline in the area's income'.[8]

If at the time the common market was relatively unimportant, it follows that it was a relatively unimportant cause of the inter-territorial inequalities. It would therefore have been an error to expect the dissolution of the common market to nullify the disequalizing forces operating in the East African economy.

Of course it is true that the absolute dependence of Kenya on the tariff preference was greater than that of Tanzania and Uganda. But it is equally true that inter-territorial exports which were independent of the preference were at a much higher level from Kenya than from the other two countries. Both facts were a reflection of the structure of the East African economy in which the productive capacity of Kenya was much more directed towards the East African market than was that of Uganda or Tanzania. This was the result of geography and of historical accident. It was also, no doubt, the result of deliberate policies in the past, such as that of encouraging European settlement in Kenya. Doubtless over a long period the customs union played a part. It may have been of considerable importance in the establishment of the infant industries which had grown out of their dependence on the preference. Nevertheless it is entirely invalid to judge the importance of the common market and its disequalizing effects from the figures of total inter-territorial trade and the nominal protection accorded by the customs tariff.

These considerations about the importance of the customs union also have a bearing on the related question of the extent to which the tariff was discriminatory between the territories. Dharam Ghai argued in an original analysis that the tariff was much more protective of Kenya's industries than of Tanzania's, so that the benefits of import substitution accrued mainly to Kenya while the costs fell mainly on Tanzania.[9] But this analysis used the nominal tariff rates, and consequently assumed that the protection accorded was 'necessary' and never 'excessive'. Commodities which, though nominally protected, would sell inter-territorially, independently of the protection, should not be included in such an analysis. The nominal tariff on these products does not measure the cost of import substitution. It may indicate a measure of monopoly profit paid by buyers in Uganda and Tanzania to producers in Kenya, but that is not the same thing. In consequence, Ghai's analysis exaggerated the discriminatory character of the tariff and the unequal distribution of the costs and benefits of import substitution.[10]

Table 5.5 shows that the protection provided was smaller, and, except in one instance, the differences in the protection provided were much less in terms of the 'necessary' than in terms of the 'nominal' degree of protection. The table is calculated from the 1962 trade statistics; the 'necessary' rate differs from the 'nominal' because the trade which it has been argued did not depend on the tariff preference (trade in milk, beer, cigarettes, and manufactures which were exported outside East Africa at average values higher than those in inter-territorial trade) are counted as having a zero protection.

An analysis of the territorial impact of the tariff which takes account of the distinction between 'necessary' and 'excessive' protection leads to the conclusion that there was relatively little difference in the degree of protection afforded to the inter-territorial trade of the three countries. In particular, the difference between the protection afforded to

Kenya's exports in Tanzania and that afforded to Tanzania's exports in Kenya was negligible. The evidence, properly assessed, does not support the view that Tanzania had lost absolutely from her membership of the common market.

TABLE 5.5

Average degree of protection of exports, per cent

	Kenya to Uganda	Uganda to Kenya	Kenya to Tanganyika	Tanganyika to Kenya	Uganda to Tanganyika	Tanganyika to Uganda
Necessary	19	9	12	11	19	10
Nominal	36	41	45	16	68	13

Source: Hazlewood, A., op. cit.

This examination of the alleged discriminatory effect of the common tariff is appropriately followed by the consideration of an analysis of the costs and benefits of the common market by W. T. Newlyn, which also appeared to show that Tanzania would be better off outside.[11] The analysis was based on the idea of the 'shiftability' of Kenya industry to Tanzania and Uganda. An industry was deemed to be shiftable to one of these countries if the average output per plant were less than the value of the industry's exports to that country. In other words, the criterion of shiftability was the scale of production in relation to the size of the market.

The average size of plant in each industry was derived from the data in the Kenya Census of Manufacturing. In fact, the categories of the census included such a diversity of products that the average output per plant, derived by dividing the total output of the 'industry' by the number of establishments, was a largely meaningless statistic. In addition, there was not only a wide dispersion in the size of establishments, but also a correlation between size and the nature of the product. Finally, the exports of an industry group were not usually a representative selection of its products. These three characteristics of the census categories are all illustrated by the beer industry. This category included the production by municipal breweries of 'African beer', *pombe*, an entirely different product from European-type beer, the main product of the industry. The average output of the industry per establishment was less than its exports to Tanzania, but this was the result of combining a large value of European-type beer, produced in a few large establishments, with an average output larger than the industry's exports to Tanzania, and the small value of *pombe* produced in a large number of establishments. Only European-type beer was exported, *pombe* being a purely locally-marketed product.

For these reasons the census categories could not properly be used to analyse the shiftability of Kenya industry. It could be demonstrated, in fact, that eleven of the fifteen industries classified on the basis of the census data as shiftable did not in fact meet the criterion of shiftability when the data were analysed in greater detail. More knowledge of any specialization of establishments on particular products might have shown that the remainder also failed to satisfy the shiftability criterion.[12]

If in the absence of the common market 'shiftable' Kenya industries would have been established in Tanzania and Uganda, it can be argued that their establishment in Kenya was a loss to these other countries from their membership of the common market. In fact, as the Kenya Census of Manufactures does not provide a proper basis for identifying the shiftable industries, any calculation of the gains and losses of the common market based largely on the census data is invalid.

The general conclusion from this examination of attempts to measure the gains and losses from the common market must be that no convincing demonstration was provided that any country had been an absolute loser. It was widely acknowledged that the benefits of the common market had been unevenly distributed, but there had been no acceptable measurement of the extent of the inequality, let alone a demonstration that any country had actually been made worse off.[13]

The benefits from economic integration derived not only from the common market but also from the common services. The distribution of the benefits of the common services could reinforce or offset the pattern of distribution of the benefits of the common market. The total expenditure of the non-self-contained services in 1964–5 was some £7·5m., but an analysis of the distribution between the territories of the benefits of the expenditure as compared with the territories' contributions concluded that there was only a small redistribution (£0·2m.) from Kenya to Tanzania and Uganda.[14] Cross-subsidization between the territories through the operation of the non-self-contained services obviously had no significant influence on the overall distribution of benefits. The redistribution through the self-contained services was probably of much greater importance, although there was very little information on which to base estimates.

In the absence of reliable information, speculation about the territorial incidence of the self-contained services has to be based on certain general considerations. It was commonly accepted as a fact that the railway services in Tanzania were unprofitable, and that there was a cross-subsidization between the Tanzania and the Kenya–Uganda lines. It was also generally acknowledged that the internal air services were subsidized from the profits on the external services. As so many of the internal services operated in Tanzania, it was not unreasonable to conclude that the Tanzanian services were subsidized. It seemed reasonable to suppose that the geography of Tanzania, and in particular the nature of the population distribution, made the postal and telecommunications services costly, so that there was some cross-subsidization of Tanzania by the remainder of East Africa on that account. One guess at an answer was that there was perhaps a cross-subsidization from Kenya and Uganda to Tanzania of some £2·5m.[15] If this figure was anything like correct, it provided a powerful counterweight to the unequal distribution of the gains from the common market.

These calculations of the cross-subsidization through the common services did not take into account the indirect benefits deriving from the expenditures carried out by the common institutions. These expenditures were highly concentrated in Kenya, and the 'multiplier effects' of the expenditures may be presumed to have provided additional benefits which increased the relative advantage to Kenya of the integration arrangements.

Estimates by R. H. Green[16] attempted to bring these indirect benefits into the assessment. Green also attempted to take an important step forward and to measure the net gains to East Africa as a whole from the greater efficiency of the services as a result of their being operated in common and of the greater efficiency of industry arising from its free access to the whole East African market. It was certainly desirable to emphasize the fact that there were net gains from integration, and that one country's gain was not necessarily another's loss. The estimates suggested that East Africa's total gain amounted to a little under 3 per cent of gross domestic product in the monetary sector, some two-thirds of the gain deriving from the common services and one-third from the common market. The importance of the indirect benefits of the expenditures of the common services gave most of the benefits of the common services to Kenya, according to this calculation. Taking account of all the effects, Green's calculations showed Kenya to benefit to the extent of nearly 9 per cent of monetary GDP, Uganda to benefit marginally, and Tanzania to lose to the extent of more than 2 per cent of monetary GDP. However, the heroic nature of some of the assumptions behind these calculations means that an agnostic position is still tenable on the question of whether any country was absolutely worse off as a result of participating in the common arrangements.

It was common ground for all observers that the short-run costs of a break-up would be high, and although there were many advocates of a more equitable distribution of the benefits of the common arrangements, no one proposed their dissolution.

NOTES

[1] An exposition of what was perhaps the analysis underlying the judgements of the Raisman Report is available in two articles by a member of the Commission, Brown, A. J., 'Economic Separatism versus a Common Market in Developing Countries', *Yorkshire B. Econ. Soc. Research*, May and Nov. 1961.

[2] Colonial Office, *East Africa: Report of the Economic and Fiscal Commission*, Cmnd 1279 (London: HMSO, 1961), paras 49–59.

[3] Massell, B. F., *East African Economic Union: An Evaluation and Some Implications for Policy* (Santa Monica: The RAND Corporation, 1963), pp. 21–3.

[4] The index is calculated as:

$$Cp = \frac{\Sigma|a-p|}{2}$$

where Cp = the index of concentration;
   a = the percentage of the total area in each administrative unit;
   p = the percentage of the total population in each administrative unit.

See Hazlewood, A., 'An Approach to the Analysis of the Spatial Distribution of the Market in East Africa', *B. Oxford Univ. Inst. Econ. Statist.*, Nov. 1969.

[5] See Hazlewood, A., op. cit., for a fuller discussion with details of the statistical analysis.

[6] Cmnd 1279, paras 51–9.

[7] Hazlewood, A., 'The East African Common Market: Importance and Effects', *B. Oxford Univ. Inst. Econ. Statist.*, Feb. 1966.

[8] Massell, B. F., op. cit. (note 3), p. 85.

[9] Ghai, D., 'Territorial Distribution of the Benefits and Costs of the East African Common Market', *East Afr. Econ. R.*, June 1964, reprinted in Leys, C., and Robson, R., *Federation in East Africa* (Nairobi: Oxford University Press, 1965).

[10] See Hazlewood, A., op. cit. (note 7).

[11] Newlyn, W. T., 'Gains and Losses in the East African Common Market', *Yorkshire B. Econ. Soc. Research*, Nov. 1965.

[12] Hazlewood, A., 'The "Shiftability" of Industry and the Measurement of Gains and Losses in the East African Common Market', *B. Oxford Univ. Inst. Econ. Statist.*, May 1966.

[13] See also the following contributions in *B. Oxford Univ. Inst. Econ. Statist.* To the discussion summarized above: Wood, R. N., Nov. 1966; Newlyn, W. T., Nov. 1966; Ghai, D., Aug. 1967; Hazlewood, A., Aug. 1967; Robson, P., May 1968.

[14] Hazlewood, A., 'The Territorial Incidence of the East African Common Services', *B. Oxford Univ. Inst. Econ. Statist.*, Aug. 1965.

[15] Hazlewood, A., op. cit.

[16] In an unpublished paper for East African Institute of Social Research, Kampala, 1964.

6 Strains and Stresses

(A) FAILINGS OF
THE INDEPENDENCE SETTLEMENT

Some of the weaknesses in the Common Services Organization which led to strained relations between the three members have been described in Chapter 4. As time passed they assumed increasing importance. The constraints imposed by the common arrangements became more irksome as the newly independent governments began to pursue more active, nationally oriented development policies. In consequence, increasing importance came to be given to the fact that there were no provisions to regulate the operation of the common market, except for the fiscal redistribution through the Distributable Pool. This redistribution was not large enough to convince Uganda and Tanzania that it produced an equitable distribution of the benefits of the common market and common services. To the other members the arrangements still seemed to contribute to the growing economic dominance of Kenya. The statistics which showed that between 1960 and 1964 the gross domestic product as a whole and of each sector of the economy expanded faster in Tanzania and Uganda than in Kenya did not convince them to the contrary. In fact, more attention was paid to the statistics of inter-territorial trade, which showed increasing surpluses for Kenya and deficits for Uganda and Tanzania. Between 1961 and 1964 Kenya's inter-territorial surplus increased from £9·0m. to £14·4m., Tanzania's deficit from £8·4m. to £10·6m., and Uganda's deficit from £0·6m. to £3·8m. These imbalances in trade were taken to demonstrate the unbalanced distribution of benefits, and the need for new policies.

The machinery for economic co-ordination provided by EACSO was weak, despite useful work of a technical nature by officials. The East African Statistical Department, which had been seen as part of the machinery of economic co-ordination, continued to produce statistics on an East African basis, but in formulating their economic policies the individual governments relied on their own statistical services, which had been established in 1961. The industrial licensing system was not being used to promote balanced development by influencing the location of industry, and applied to a few industries only. There was no co-ordination of policies to prevent uneconomic duplication of other industries. Tanzania maintained the hope that industrial licensing could be used to 'correct' the imbalances in industrial development, and in 1964 an agreement was reached (backed by a threat of withdrawal from the common market by Tanzania) to regulate the common market in this way.

(B) THE KAMPALA AGREEMENT

The original agreement was reached between ministers of the three countries in April 1964, at Kampala. Further talks were held and a modified agreement was approved by a meeting of Heads of State held at Mbale in January 1965. Although versions of the agreement were made public,[1] it was never officially published as a tripartite document, and the formulation of the legal convention or treaty in which the principles of agreement were to have been set out was overtaken by events in the middle of 1965.

Concern about the inequalities in development had somehow been transformed by the time of the Kampala Agreement into a concern about imbalances in inter-territorial trade, and agreement was reached at Kampala on ways to reduce them. There were five ways in which it was agreed the imbalances of inter-territorial trade could be righted. In summary, in the order in which it was thought they could be applied, the measures agreed upon were: (*i*) to arrange a shift in the territorial distribution of production by a number of firms which operated in two or more of the countries; (*ii*) to institute quotas on inter-territorial trade; (*iii*) to allocate certain major industries between the countries; (*iv*) to increase sales from a country in deficit in inter-territorial trade to a country in surplus; and (*v*) to devise a system of inducements and allocations of industry to secure an equitable distribution of industrial development between the three countries.

Action was immediately taken on the first of these five measures, which was to persuade certain firms which operated in each country to increase their production in Tanzania so as to import less from Kenya. The products concerned were cigarettes, beer, shoes, and cement. Similar action was envisaged between Kenya and Uganda, but was made less easy by the fact that the inter-territorial firms either did not then operate in Uganda (shoes and cement) or were not the sole firm producing the commodity (beer).

The East African Tobacco Company was already planning an expansion of its production in Dar es Salaam, and would be manufacturing only small runs of specialist brands for inter-territorial trade.

The Bata Shoe Company specialized in its factories, and did not dupli-cate production in its different factories. It would be introducing a new line at Dar es Salaam, but this would still leave a substantial imbalance between Kenya and Tanzania. A cement plant was under construction in Dar es Salaam, and it was agreed that the firm should be asked to bring forward the completion date. The expansion and re-equipment of the Dar es Salaam brewery was also planned, as was an expansion of the Moshi brewery. When carried out these plans would largely eliminate trade between Kenya and Tanzania in the products of East African Breweries (and its associates). It was estimated that the action en-visaged for these four products would reduce the trade imbalance between Kenya and Tanzania by £1·8m., or 24 per cent of the 1963 figure.

The second most important attack on the trade imbalance, in terms of the likely speed of its effect, was the decision to institute quotas on exports from surplus to deficit countries. The governments agreed on:

> The application of a system of quotas and suspended quotas whereby exports from the surplus countries would be progressively reduced, and local production increased in the deficit countries according to the building up of the productive capacity of the deficit country.

A quota was to be applied where there was existing productive capacity in the deficit country, and a suspended quota where the deficit country was proposing to develop productive capacity.

The quota system was not imbued with an excessively restrictionist spirit. It allowed a deficit country to apply for new quotas against a surplus country only if its overall imbalance with the surplus country amounted to more than 20 per cent of its total exports to that country. Quotas could be imposed only 'provided that a firm could operate on an economically viable basis or expand its operations within the national market'. It was noted that 'considerable administrative care would be required in reducing the size of a quota by stages as a firm came into production in order to ensure the maintenance of East African output'. It was recognized that 'it would be mutually beneficial to adopt a more flexible attitude towards inter-territorial trade imbalances in particular commodities once the aggregate inter-territorial trade imbalances had been eliminated'. And it was agreed that the quota system was not to be a permanent feature of the common market, but was intended only to assist in redressing trade imbalances. It would not apply to the products of industries allocated under the Agreement. The determination of which industries could reasonably be included in the quota system was one of the tasks of a Committee of Industrial Experts, the establishment of which was part of the Kampala Agreement.

By mistake the original formula for calculating the size of a quota would have had a highly restrictionist effect, and the error was corrected in the revised agreement. The revised agreement also took account of the possibility that quotas would have the effect of diverting a deficit country's purchases from a surplus country to a source outside East Africa. To institute a system which resulted in a transfer of purchases from Kenya to non-East African suppliers would have violated the whole purpose of the quota system and the spirit of the Kampala Agreement, and the revised agreement stated that:

the Governments, in a desire to minimize the impact of quotas to the extent possible within the objectives of this agreement, agree to take external trade factors into account when calculating the size of the quotas, so long as this does not cause delays.

Whatever the intention, the arrangements initiated under the Kampala Agreement had some restrictive and cost-raising effects. The quota on beer exports from Kenya to Tanzania restricted trade by more than Tanzanian production was immediately able to substitute; there was a net shortfall in the supply in Tanzania of high-quality beers from East African sources, with a consequent switch to imports from outside East Africa. The cigarette manufacturers had to incur considerable expense in shifting the weight of their production from Kenya to Tanzania. The establishment of the Dar es Salaam cement plant (agreed upon before the Kampala Agreement) would leave all three countries with a considerable excess capacity in cement. Territorial self-sufficiency undoubtedly imposes costs. The costs are worth while if they are a cost of maintaining the main structure of the common market, and not a stage towards the general reduction in inter-territorial trade in the interest of territorial self-sufficiency.

That the Kampala Agreement did not envisage such general self-sufficiency is of course evident from its proposals for the allocation of new industries between the territories and from its proposals for a committee of industrial experts to determine in which products self-sufficiency was, and in which it was not, harmful to the interests of East Africa.

The other three measures agreed at Kampala could not have such immediate effects as those already discussed, though two of them at any rate were directed at the underlying problem, the inequalities in development, rather than at the symptom, the imbalances of trade. First of all, a territorial allocation of a number of major industries was agreed upon. Electric light bulbs were to be manufactured in Kenya; bicycle parts and nitrogenous fertilizers in Uganda; radio assembly and manufacture, and the manufacture of motor tyres and tubes, were to be located in Tanzania. The original agreement allocated some vehicle assembly to Tanganyika, but in the revised agreement no mention was made of this industry, and 'aluminium foil, circles and plain sheets' had been substituted as allocated to Tanzania. The industries concerned would be scheduled under the territorial Industrial Licensing Acts and the governments would arrange with the East African Industrial Council that an exclusive licence would be given to a firm operating in the agreed territory. The measures under this head were potentially the most important and constructive aspects of the Kampala Agreement. If they worked they would provide a way of maintaining the benefits of the common market while offsetting its disequalizing tendencies. It may be that the locations resulting from the allocation would be less efficient than those that would be chosen in the absence of the agreement, and it seems unlikely that the costs of different locations were an element in the decision on the territorial allocation of these industries. Against this, however, must be set the more efficient scale of operation that would be secured by tariff-free access to the whole East African market. It is fairly certain that the balance of advantage was with the agreement. The most efficient location, if it involved concentration at the most developed centre, as it probably would for most industries, could not be obtained together with the economies of access to the common market. A more equal spread of development was a minimum necessary condition for the maintenance of the common market (though not necessarily a sufficient condition). Fiscal compensations avoid the costs of inefficient location, but are not an acceptable substitute for development. The cost of a relatively less efficient location was the price of the maintenance of the common market.

The trouble with the policy of industrial allocation embodied in the Kampala Agreement was that the industries might not have come to East Africa at all. The agreement divided the catch before it was caught. It is admitted in the agreement that 'it is not possible to say when any of these units will come into production'. One may also wonder what would be the response of government X if an industrialist wanted to establish an industry in X, but would not establish it in East Africa at all if (because of the allocations of the Kampala Agreement) he were allowed only to establish it in country Y. The government of X would have to be very strong-minded to refuse the industry; and one may wonder if Y and Z would not be wise to allow the industry to be established in X rather than not to have it in East Africa at all.

The industrial allocation policy of the Kampala Agreement was not, therefore, without its difficulties. Nevertheless, an agreement to take deliberate measures to reduce the inequalities between the territories while maintaining the advantages of the common market was warmly to be welcomed.

The remaining measures agreed upon were, first, that surplus countries would endeavour to increase their purchases from deficit countries, and second, that 'future allocation of industry and differential incentives to industry' should be referred to a committee of industrial experts.

The Industrial Experts Committee had, first, to draw up a list of 'East African industries', defined as those which to be economically feasible required access to the entire East African market, or at least to a market larger than that of any single East African country. Secondly, the Committee was to examine 'the basis for distribution of these industries' having regard to the economic feasibility of different locations, to the need for an equitable territorial distribution of industry, and to the necessary 'measures for achieving rapidly an equitable pattern of industrial location'.

The work of the Committee of Industrial Experts would have had to provide the rationale for a long-term pursuit of the aims of the Kampala Agreement. Without the studies which it was planned that the committee should carry out, the agreement was no more than an *ad hoc* arrangement to meet an emergency situation. In fact, the Committee of Industrial Experts was never set up, and as an adjunct of the Kampala Agreement it ceased to be of relevance with the effective demise of the agreement in 1965. This is not to say, of course, that the inter-territorial planning of industrial location, which was the positive and constructive part of the Kampala Agreement, ceased to be of relevance to the East African situation.

(C) SEPARATE CURRENCIES

The Kampala Agreement had been received as an agreement to keep in being the common market. The next news of economic relations between the territories was the announcement that each country was to establish its own central bank and issue its own currency.

The East African shilling had circulated in the territories since 1920. With a single currency the territories constituted a full monetary union. The Board issued currency only in exchange for sterling at the fixed rate of exchange, but the currency issue could expand to match requirements of the total money supply as determined by the advances of the commercial banks. The expatriate character of the banking system ensured that the domestic money supply was not restricted by a sterling shortage. At most times, indeed, the East African banking system had excess supplies of sterling, though during 1960, when there were large outflows of capital on non-banking private accounts, the expatriate banks imported funds.[2]

The system was certainly restrictive when a 100 per cent external reserve was imposed, in the sense that deficit financing was impossible. But it was permissible from 1955 to depart from the 100 per cent external reserve which had previously been the rule. At first a £10m. fiduciary issue was allowed. This figure was later raised to £20m. and then, in 1963, to £25m. In addition there was an allowance for temporary crop-finance, which had been increased from £5m. to £10m. at the end of 1962. The total permitted fiduciary issue was divided between the territories in proportion to the estimated territorial distribution of the currency circulation. The total issue was never near the maximum, though at times a particular territory approached its limits (Uganda in

December 1961, and Tanganyika in December 1962). On those occasions it was a temporary phenomenon associated with the purchase
by the Board of Treasury bills, not of long-term securities, and the
Board had envisaged the temporary transfer of unused fiduciary powers
between the territories.

The Currency Board responded to developments in East Africa and
'deliberately set out, within the limits of present possibilities, to provide
facilities and carry out tasks normally attributed to central banks'. The
Board declared:

> Its aim has been to bridge the gap of time and opportunity between
> the old system and the creation of a central bank in conditions which
> allow it to operate fully and effectively in East Africa's interest and
> preserve one currency for the area.[3]

The Board pointed out that, by agreement, it already had wide freedom
of action, and was in fact much less circumscribed than many central
banks. It acts as:

> a banker to the banks, and it must be emphasized that it already acts
> as a lender of last resort to them. It does so by being continuously
> ready to rediscount territorial Treasury Bills where available and
> through its crop finance facilities . . . No limits are in sight here
> beyond the Board's ceiling (which could be raised) and beyond its
> own policy towards applicants.

There had, nevertheless, for some time been a growing recognition of
the desirability of a central bank in East Africa, but official steps to
establish an East African central bank had been inhibited by political
considerations. Before independence for the three countries was clearly
foreseen, one of the fears was of establishing new institutions in which
settler-dominated Kenya might have a predominant say.[4] The independence of Tanganyika and the prospect of the imminent independence
of Uganda and Kenya eliminated this particular fear, and more official
attention came to be given to the matter. However, the countries could
not agree on a central banking structure, and eventually, the International Monetary Fund was asked to advise on the form a central
banking system should take.

The problem in determining the structure of an East African central
bank was that of deciding how centralized a structure should be
established, and to devise a system which would work in the absence
of a common government in East Africa. The Currency Board expressed
the view that given the complexities of the East African situation the
operation of a central bank would be difficult in the absence of some
form of central political direction, so that a political federation provided the best assurance for a successful transition to full central
banking. Federation was not, however, assumed in the different proposals for central banking. One scheme[5] had a single central bank,
which, with the sole right of currency issue, would ultimately determine

monetary policy, including the size and distribution of the fiduciary issue. In addition, a state bank would be established in each country. In this scheme the real power would reside with the central bank. Another scheme[6] was much less centralized: each country would have its own central bank issuing its own currency, with co-ordination between the banks being achieved by an East African Reserve Board.

Both these schemes were criticized as being unstable compromises.[7] It was argued that the first was not far removed from a central bank with branches. Under it essential authority would still rest in the central board of governors and the system would simply operate at higher costs because of duplication, and as the state banks offered a misleading suggestion of independent authority there would be a ready framework for disputes. The second scheme, on the other hand, was much closer to a system of completely separate central banks, and would rapidly deteriorate into it.

The possibility of unilateral action by Tanzania had existed for some time. Two or three years before the decision was announced it had been rumoured that Tanganyika was to issue her own currency. Similar rumours were abroad early in 1965, and in June 1965, without the IMF recommendations having been made public, it was announced in the budget speeches that the countries were to establish separate central banks and to issue separate currencies.

(D) THE TREND TO DISSOLUTION

Paradoxically, the trend towards the dissolution of the common arrangements stemmed from a movement for closer association. By the time the Common Services Organization was established the question of federation had again become a live issue. As recently as 1953 the threat of an imposed federation, as it was thought to be, had led to a furore in Uganda, to the deportation of the Kabaka of Buganda, and to a campaign of civil disobedience. With the subsequent constitutional changes and the impending independence of all three territories, federation had become a symbol not of settler domination but of African unity.

The future President Nyerere had offered to delay the independence of Tanganyika so that all three territories could enter the East African federation at the same time as independent states. That was not to be, and Tanganyika achieved independence in December 1961 and Uganda in October 1962. In June 1963, when it was clear that Kenya would become independent within a few months, the political leaders of the three countries issued a declaration pledging themselves to 'the political Federation of East Africa'.[8] The declaration stated that 'the East Africa High Commission and its successor the Common Services Organization have taught us the value of links in the economic field', and remarked that 'an important factor in view of our determination to achieve Federation is the existence of shared currency; a leading aspect of economic working together is the functioning of the E.A. Common Market'. The difficulty with existing arrangements, it was argued, was that they lacked central political direction: 'We are convinced that the time has now come to create such central political authority.'

The declaration envisaged a timetable for negotiations between the countries which would result in the establishment of the federation by the end of the year. The proposal for so rapid a result was undoubtedly in part a tactic to ensure that there was no delay in Kenya's achieving independence, and that was successful, for Kenya became independent in December. In other respects the aims of the declaration were not realized. Difficulties arose in the Working Party that had been set up to devise the federal constitution, and it soon became apparent that the issues were far too complicated to be settled by the end of 1963. In fact, by early 1964 it had become clear that federation was, to say the least, not imminent.

The concentration of attention on federation had led to a neglect of any possibilities for improved economic co-ordination available within the framework of EACSO. The failure of the movement for federation left fully exposed the inadequacies of EACSO for a country which wished to regulate the operation of the common market to achieve more balanced development. As a temporary arrangement, soon to be superseded by a federal structure within which equalizing policies could be actively promoted, EACSO was acceptable. With the fading prospect of federation, Tanzania in particular began to insist on changes being instituted in the inter-territorial arrangements, if she was not to withdraw from them. The Kampala Agreement was an attempt to meet the need and to hold the common market together but was followed, as we have seen, by the decision to establish separate currencies. The decision on the currency was not the first example of the dissolution of common arrangements. In 1961 Tanganyika had withdrawn from the East African Navy, because it was based in Mombasa and did not, she believed, contribute to her defence. In 1963 Uganda withdrew from the East African Tourist Travel Association, on the grounds that her contribution to its cost was disproportionate to the benefit she received. The break-up of the University of East Africa into three separate universities was also being talked about. But the decision on the currency was so striking a departure from the common arrangements that it was interpreted as the 'death knell of the East African common market'.[9]

The announcements about the impending break-up of the single-currency area provided the occasion for a good deal of recrimination. Kenya put the blame for the dissolution on the other countries, and particularly on Tanzania. 'They refused to listen to me,' the Minister of Finance said, 'and they also told me that they were determined to have their own way in issuing their own currencies.'[10] Tanzania did not deny that the dissolution of the currency area was at her instigation. Her Minister of Finance is reported to have said that Tanzania had not deliberately sought to break up the monetary area, but the failure of the federation talks made a single central banking system impossible. The Minister said:

> In the interests of East African unity we have waited and discussed for four years before taking any action to dismantle the East African Currency Board and to transfer the authority to the Government. This is a very great sacrifice for any country and particularly for a developing country which is anxious to promote the development of its own monetary institutions.[11]

Kenya took no retaliatory action, though her Minister of Finance was reported to have predicted that all East Africa's economic links would collapse if the present trend continued, and in his budget speech he said that 'the decision which the Tanzanian Government has taken will obviously have wide implications on the structure of the common market and the Common Services Organization'. The Prime Minister of Uganda, on the other hand, was quoted as saying that 'East African co-operation is not dependent on the common currency and Tanzania's decision is not going to affect the common services'.[12] Although at the time this seemed an unduly optimistic view, the arrangements that had been agreed between the countries suggests that it was a correct analysis. It had been agreed that the three currencies should remain freely convertible at the par rate of exchange and that there should be co-operation between the monetary authorities to ensure that these conditions were maintained. The currencies would therefore be separate currencies in only a very limited sense, and their existence would impose no serious complications in the operations of the common services or the common market. It might seem, therefore, that the adverse effect of the currency break-up on the common market and common services would arise more from the general emphasis on territorial interests, and on impatience with the limitations imposed by the inter-territorial arrangements, of which the currency break-up was a symptom, rather than from the difficulty of working the common arrangements in the absence of a common currency.

However, the less optimistic view would have seemed to be realistic to those who wondered if the agreed conditions would be long maintained. If the creation of separate currencies had been undertaken because the constraints imposed by the common currency were irksome, the constraints imposed by the agreement to maintain convertibility at a fixed exchange-rate between the currencies would be likely to prove equally irksome. The dissolution of the common currency might then be proved to have been the first step towards exchange control on inter-territorial transactions, the abandonment of the par values of the currencies, and restrictions on inter-territorial trade for foreign-exchange reasons. But that was looking ahead, and the more immediately adverse effects on economic co-operation in East Africa arose from restrictions on trade rather than from the creation of separate currencies.

The quota committee established under the Kampala Agreement was pursuing its deliberations when unilateral action on the part of Tanzania was announced. In the middle of June, Tanzania imposed restrictions on a wide range of imports from Kenya. These restrictions went much further than had been envisaged in the agreement, and it was by no means clear that Tanzania was immediately in a position to substitute domestic products for the displaced imports from Kenya. It may be that in part the restrictions were intended to establish a bargaining position, to encourage firms to leap the barrier and to establish productive capacity in Tanzania. This might well be thought legitimate in Tanzania's position, but in the absence of the information that was to be provided by the Industrial Experts Committee it would be essentially an unplanned process, likely to impose substantial costs and inefficiency on the industries affected. Those with large economies of scale would be unlikely to respond to the encouragement. But it was not improbable that the restrictions would result in the existence of a larger number of less efficient plants in East Africa than would otherwise be established.

It is unlikely that the revenue-allocation arrangements would have long survived the imposition of these restrictions on trade. The Kenya Minister of Finance was reported as saying that 'Kenya had been paying 50 per cent of the cost of the common services, but if Tanzania and Uganda were to continue to restrict Kenya imports, Kenya would not contribute so much as it had been contributing in the past'.[13] If Tanzania was taking direct steps to offset Kenya's gains from the common market, Kenya might well have come to feel that she should not continue with the fiscal redistribution.

From Tanzania's point of view, to the extent that the restrictions caused a diversion of her imports from Kenya to outside sources her customs revenue would rise and she would automatically pay more into the Distributable Pool, thus reducing the fiscal distribution in her favour. The restrictions on Kenya's trade would reduce the profitability of Kenya companies, and the efforts in Tanzania to stimulate industrial development would lead to a rise in the total of industrial profits generated in Tanzania. On both counts there would be a fall in Kenya's and a rise in Tanzania's contribution to the Distributable Pool from income tax on companies. On this account too, therefore, the redistribution in Tanzania's favour through the Pool would be reduced, and might have led Tanzania to feel that she would do better to withdraw from the pooling arrangement.

The Kampala Agreement must be considered an early victim of the inter-territorial trade restrictions outside the scope of the agreement. They could not but lead to an abandonment of any agreement on the location of industry and to vigorous competition between the countries to obtain new industries within their borders. It could be said that in any case the agreement was ended by the decision to establish separate currencies, for Kenya accepted the agreement on condition that the common currency was maintained. It has also been argued that Kenya's unwillingness to schedule under the Industrial Licensing Act the industries allocated to the other countries, and her failure to ratify the agreement formally, brought it to an end.

It may be seen as a paradox that Tanzania, the strongest proponent and initiator of proposals for East African federation, should have initiated the dissolution of the common arrangements. The paradox, in fact, is more apparent than real. The apparent reversal of Tanzanian attitudes is understandable. With the formation of a federal government Tanzania would have had hopes of a vigorous development policy for East Africa as a whole, with the equalizing allocations of finance and investment which are possible in a federation. The Tanzanian Finance Minister was essentially right to argue that, with the failure of the federation talks, Tanzania had to look to her own development policies. And it was natural enough to find that those policies were inhibited by the inter-territorial arrangements. In East Africa these were more or less satisfactory in 'the era of colonialism'; they were quite unsatisfactory for 'the era of development'.

It would be a mistake to conclude from this fact that a dissolution of the common arrangements could have been viewed with equanimity. It would have been a mistake to think that the creation of the central banks could make more than a modest contribution to economic development. The scope for expansionary monetary measures was severely limited by two interrelated factors: the rapid effect of expansionary policies on the balance of payments; and the limited extent to which there existed diversified excess productive capacity to allow output to respond in the short period to increases in demand. Secondly, it would have been a mistake to think that a break-up of the common market would have benefited Tanzania and Uganda. A great deal of the relative backwardness of their economies could not be blamed on the common market, and a withdrawal from the common market would not have neutralized the disadvantages under which they laboured. The dissolution of the common market, given the small size of the economies of Tanzania and Uganda, would not have diverted much industrial development to them from Kenya, though it would have been likely significantly to reduce the future rate of industrial growth in East Africa as a whole. Even though by the middle 1960s the common market had not been of major importance in the industrial development that had occurred in East Africa, as the Raisman Commission had argued, 'the contributions which the Common Market arrangements can make to economic growth are likely to be greater in the future than in the past'.[14] And it did not follow that future economic growth on the basis of the common market would necessarily intensify and perpetuate the relative backwardness of Tanzania and Uganda. Even before the Kampala Agreement the balance of industrial development showed signs of change. Ghai pointed out that,[15] despite the losses which in his view she had sustained in the past, it might not be in Tanzania's interest to withdraw from the common market because:

> A number of industries have been started there recently which will rely substantially on the East African market for their sales; and therefore even if Tanganyika has not gained from the Common Market in the past, there is no reason to believe that she will not do so in the future.

It would have been ironical if the common market had disintegrated because of an exaggerated view of its importance in the past just at a time when it could begin to play a major part in the industrialization of East Africa.

The trend towards disintegration which was increasingly evident during 1965 was not accepted with complacency by the three governments. At the end of June, Kenya gave formal notice under the Common Services Agreement calling for a review of the agreement and for discussions on all aspects of economic co-operation. It came to be accepted that a long, hard look at the inter-territorial arrangements was essential if they were to survive. The Heads of State, meeting in Mombasa at the end of August, determined to establish a commission on the common market and common services. It was not to be an expert commission of inquiry – another Raisman Commission – but was to consist of three ministers from each country together with an independent chairman. The commission, under the chairmanship of Professor Kjeld Philip, did not get under way effectively until January 1966. Despite this unexpectedly late start, before the middle of May the Commission, with the assistance of a formidable team of advisers mainly recruited by the United Nations Economic Commission for Africa, was able to submit a report covering the whole range of inter-territorial economic questions. This report formed the basis for the Treaty for East African Co-operation.

NOTES

[1] The original Agreement was published as a pamphlet by the Tanzanian Information Service; the revised version was published unofficially in the *East African Journal* (Nairobi), April 1965.

[2] See Newlyn, W. T., and Rowan, D. C., *Money and Banking in British Colonial Africa* (Oxford: Clarendon Press, 1954), and Hazlewood, A., 'The Economics of Colonial Monetary Arrangements', *Soc. Econ. Studies*, Dec. 1954.

[3] East African Currency Board, *Report for the Year ended 30th June 1963*.

[4] See McWilliam, M. D., 'Is there a Case for an East African Central Bank?', *East Afr. Econ. R.*, Jan. 1959.

[5] Blumenthal, E., *Tanganyika – East Africa: The Present Monetary System and its Future* (Dar es Salaam: Government Printer, 1963).

[6] Newlyn, W. T., 'Monetary Systems and Integration', *East Afr. Econ. R.*, June 1964. Professor Newlyn was Economic Adviser to the Government of Uganda at the time, and the argument of the article may be taken as indicating the lines of his proposals to the Uganda Government.

[7] Clark, P. G., 'The Role of a Central Bank in Accelerating Economic Development', in East African Institute of Social and Cultural Affairs, *Problems of Economic Development in East Africa* (Nairobi: East African Publishing House, 1965).

[8] The Federation Declaration of 5 June 1963 is reproduced in Leys, C., and Robson, R., *Federation in East Africa* (Nairobi: Oxford University Press, 1965).

[9] Headline in the *Sunday Times* (London).

[10] Reported in *The Times* (London), 12 June 1965. Uganda Ministers, however, were reported (*Reporter* [Nairobi], 2 July 1965) as saying that Uganda had been forced into the currency split.

[11] *Reporter* (Nairobi), 18 June 1965.

[12] *Kenya Weekly News* (Nairobi), 25 June 1965.

[13] *Reporter* (Nairobi), 2 July 1965.

[14] Colonial Office, *East Africa: Report of the Economic and Fiscal Commission*, Cmnd 1279 (London: HMSO, 1961) para. 191(v).

[15] Ghai, D., 'Territorial Distribution of the Benefits and Costs of the East African Common Market', *East Afr. Econ. R.*, June 1964, p.40, reprinted in Leys, C., and Robson, R., op cit. (note 8).

7 The Treaty for East African Co-operation [1]

(A) INTRODUCTION

The terms of reference of the Commission established under the chairmanship of Professor Kjeld Philip were the following:

> to examine existing arrangements in East Africa for co-operation between Kenya, Tanzania and Uganda on matters of mutual interest, and having due regard to the views of the respective Governments, to make agreed recommendations on the following matters:

> (*i*) How the East African Common Market can be maintained and strengthened and the principles on which, and the manner in which, the Common Market can in future be controlled and regulated.

> (*ii*) The arrangements necessary for effective operation of the Common Market consequential upon the establishment of separate currencies.

> (*iii*) The extent to which services at present maintained in common between the three countries can be continued, and the form which such services should take.

> (*iv*) The extent to which (if at all) new services can be provided in common between the three countries, and the form which such services should take.

> (*v*) The manner in which the common services should be financed.

> (*vi*) The extent to which the management of different services can be located in different parts of East Africa.

> (*vii*) The legal, administrative and constitutional arrangements most likely to promote effective co-operation between the East African countries in the light of the recommendations made under paragraphs (*i*) (*ii*) (*iii*) (*iv*) (*v*) (*vi*).

It will be seen that the whole range of issues between the countries was open for consideration (apart from the question of political federation), though it is important to note that the dissolution of the common market was not a recommendation which the terms of reference would have allowed the Commission to make.

The Philip Commission, with its formal title, which it invented for itself, of the Commission on East African Co-operation, was not the normal kind of commission in which a group of experts is asked to examine a problem and submit a report for the consideration of government. The Commission was in fact a vehicle for negotiation between the three governments, and consisted of three ministers from each country, with an independent chairman to act not so much as umpire, but as initiator of ideas and conciliator. It is for this reason that there is no public document entitled 'The Philip Report', as there is 'The Raisman Report'. The only public document is the Treaty for East Africa Co-operation. The Commission began its deliberations towards the end of 1965, and it submitted a report to the East African governments in May 1966. There were further negotiations during the next year on the basis of this report and of drafts giving legal expression to the agreed decisions of the governments. The Treaty was signed in June 1967 by the three Heads of State, and came into effect on 1 December of that year.

All in all, it can be said that the negotiations leading to the conclusion of the Treaty, if not rapid, at least were speedier than might have been expected, given the range of issues considered and the extent to which differences had developed between the governments over the preceding years. It may be that progress was facilitated by agreement to continue much of what already existed, because in many respects the Treaty in effect confirmed and codified existing arrangements. What certainly did help was the fact that ministers and officials of each country knew a good deal about the rest of East Africa, and they knew their counterparts in the other states. Nevertheless, the conclusion of the Treaty was an encouraging demonstration of the willingness of the three countries to work together and of their fear of the consequences of splitting apart. This is not, of course, to say that the Treaty resolved all problems: in some respects it papered over the cracks in the edifice of co-operation rather than properly filling them in.

The Treaty deals with all fields of co-operation between the East African countries and establishes 'an East African Community and, as an integral part of such Community, an East African Common Market' of the three partner states, Tanzania, Uganda, and Kenya. The Treaty[2] proclaims the aim of the Community to be:

> to strengthen and regulate the industrial, commercial and other relations of the Partner States to the end that there shall be accelerated, harmonious and balanced development and sustained expansion of economic activities the benefits whereof shall be equitably shared.

(B) THE COMMON MARKET

Although the Treaty declares that 'By this Treaty the Contracting Parties establish among themselves . . . an East African Common Market,' in fact, in terms of the customary parlance, it does nothing of the kind. It does establish a customs union for manufactures, temporarily modified by a system of taxes on inter-state transfers, but there is no provision for the freedom of factor movements. There is no reference in the Treaty to the 'right of establishment', nor to the movement of labour between the partner states. There is a reference to the movement of capital, but to provide for its control, not to guarantee its freedom. The term 'common market' had been applied for so long to the East African arrangements, which were at one time properly so described, that the niceties of terminology escaped the draftsmen of the Treaty.

The Treaty required quota restrictions on inter-state trade in East African manufactures to be abolished not later than the date on which it came into force. Although freedom of trade in East African produce is envisaged, the Treaty allows a state to restrict imports of foreign produce coming to it through another partner state. This can be seen as a necessary provision to prevent easy evasion of a state's import restrictions. But it also gives authority for Tanzania to direct her imports through Tanzanian ports, restricting her imports through Mombasa, and for Uganda to require her imports to be cleared through customs in Uganda, restricting the important entrepôt activities in Mombasa and Nairobi.

Restrictions are permitted on inter-state trade in certain products which are the subject of contractual obligations by one or other of the partner states, and on certain agricultural products.

The Treaty applies to Tanzania as a whole, and there are no special provisions for Zanzibar. Zanzibar had always been outside the East African customs area, and the Treaty brought her nominally into the common arrangements.

It is the aim of the Treaty to regulate the operation of the so-called common market so as to achieve an equitable distribution of benefits between the partner states. Two new regulatory measures are introduced: a system of 'transfer taxes' and an East African Development Bank.

(C) TRANSFER TAXES

Under the transfer-tax system it is possible for the industrially less-developed countries to impose what is in effect a tariff on imports of manufactures from the relatively more developed in order to protect their own manufacturing industries. Transfer taxes can be imposed only by a country with an overall deficit in intra-East African trade in manufactures, and only on imports from a country with which it has a deficit. The prevailing pattern of intra-East African trade in manufactures at the time of the Treaty gave Tanzania a deficit with each of the other countries, and Uganda a deficit with Kenya. When the Treaty came into force, Tanzania was therefore able to impose transfer taxes on imports from both Kenya and Uganda, Uganda was able to impose them on imports from Kenya, and Kenya was not entitled to impose any transfer taxes.

The relevance of the balance of trade between the states, with its bilateralist overtones, could reasonably be questioned. The adoption of this criterion is more understandable if it is seen against the background of the public discussion in the period before the appointment of the Philip Commission, in which great emphasis was laid on the balances in inter-state trade as indicating the distribution of the benefits of the common market (*see* Chapter 6). Nevertheless, to enshrine a bilateral trade-balance criterion in the Treaty might seem to reflect a rather low degree of economic literacy. In fact, it was not quite as bad as that. The Treaty uses the inter-state trade balance in manufactures as a proxy measure for the level of industrial development in each of the partner states. Admittedly, it is not a very good proxy, but it is probably as good as any other measure that was available. The Treaty is really concerned to allow the less industrially developed partners to impose transfer taxes to protect their own production, and to increase their attractiveness as a location for manufacturing industry. This, not the trade balance, is the important point.

As the purpose of the transfer-tax system is to foster domestic production, a country is not permitted to impose transfer taxes 'across the board' on all manufactures imported from a partner with which it is in deficit. Tanzania and Uganda are not able to tax all their manufactured imports from Kenya. They can tax only those types of goods which they have a capacity to produce themselves (or will have within three months of the imposition of a tax) on a significant scale (15 per cent of the domestic consumption of the goods in the year before the imposition of the tax or a value of output of £100,000). An additional restriction is that a country cannot impose transfer taxes on a value of imports greater than its deficit, as most recently recorded, with the country whose goods it is taxing. Once it is taxing this value of imports it can impose no further transfer taxes, although existing taxes do not have to be removed.

The rate of transfer tax on any product is within the discretion of the tax-imposing country, but it may not exceed 50 per cent of the external tariff on that product. For many products this meant at the time of the Treaty that the maximum rate of transfer tax was 15–20 per cent of the product's value at its point of entry into the importing country. The transfer-tax system was conceived as a temporary device: no individual tax can continue for longer than a period of eight years, and the system comes to an end after fifteen years. Its working was to be reviewed after five years.

The imposition of a transfer tax by, say, Uganda on imports from Kenya will raise the price of Kenya goods in the Uganda market in relation not only to Uganda products but also to imports from outside East Africa. There would therefore be a tendency for imports from outside East Africa to increase at the expense of imports from Kenya. Such a diversion of trade would be incompatible with the aims of the Treaty, and the tax-imposing State is required to correct a deviation in trade if it occurs as a result of the imposition of a transfer tax. There is no reference in the Treaty to the method to be used to correct a deviation.

If an industry protected by a transfer tax manages to develop exports to the remainder of East Africa, or to other countries, equal to 30 per cent of its total sales, then the transfer tax must be removed. The argument for this rule is presumably that an industry able to export is not in need of protection. The existence of the transfer tax could itself facilitate exporting by the protected industry, because it would enable the industry to sell at a higher price at home than abroad. Price discrimination between the partner states is prohibited, but it is not disallowed in outside markets, so that the transfer taxes could provide some help, say, to Tanzania in exporting to Zambia, though this is not likely to be of much importance in practice. It might be thought more important that a protected industry does not lose its protection until it is able to export as much as 30 per cent of its output. It might seem unreasonable that, for instance, an industry in Tanzania could be exporting as much as that of its output to Kenya, and still be protected in its home market by the transfer tax. In reality, under these circumstances it would not matter much to the Kenya competitors whether a transfer tax was imposed or not. So long as price discrimination is prohibited, a Tanzanian industry able to compete in Kenya would almost certainly be competitive within the Tanzanian market without the protection of the transfer tax, so that the tax would not adversely affect the market for Kenya goods.

The treaty provides for the transfer-tax system to be operated by the East African Customs and Excise Department and for the costs of administering the taxes to be borne by the countries imposing them. It says nothing more about how the system is to be administered, although it does provide for the taxes to be based on the value of the goods at the border between the exporting and importing countries, which rules out the administration of the tax as a sales tax at retail level. When the transfer taxes were introduced their collection was associated with the Transfer Form system which already operated, and the assessment and payment of the transfer taxes became part of this procedure. In addition, customs posts were established at the borders – which were an innovation in East Africa, and a somewhat paradoxical symbol of closer co-operation. It should be noted that in the past there was no incentive to evade or falsify the transfer returns. The association of the transfer tax with the Transfer-Form procedure supplied such an incentive. The introduction of significant errors into the returns would be a matter of some importance, for it is not only the statistics of trade which derive from these returns, but also the distribution of customs revenues between the countries.

A rationalization of the thinking behind the transfer-tax system might be expressed in the following propositions:

(i) Some industries can operate efficiently in a market no larger than that of the smallest of the individual partner states's markets.

(ii) The development of these industries in each of the individual partner states is inhibited by competition from the more developed partner states: in Tanzania it is inhibited by competition from Kenyan and Ugandan firms, and in Uganda it is inhibited by competition from Kenyan firms.

(iii) Temporary protection of these industries in the less-developed partner states will enable them to survive and grow up, so that when the temporary protection accorded under the Treaty comes to an end they can properly be subjected to free competition within the whole East African market. Such competition will improve efficiency without polarizing the development of industry.

(iv) There are other industries which cannot operate efficiently within markets as small as those of the individual partner states, but which could operate efficiently within the whole East African market. Such industries will be unaffected by the transfer-tax system. They will not be subject to transfer tax in whichever country they locate, because the limitation of the market would prevent a second plant from being established if one already existed in East Africa, and to be permitted to impose a transfer tax on a product, the tax-imposing state must itself be producing the product.

(v) With the development of 'national' industries in the initially less-developed partner states under the protection of the transfer taxes, the relative attractiveness of the different partner states for these large scale 'East African' industries will become equalized, so that by the time the transfer-tax system comes to an end the partner states will be able to operate on equal footing within a full 'common market of market economies'.

An important weakness in this theoretical basis for the transfer taxes is its assumption that a clear distinction can be made between 'national' and 'East African' industries, and that the transfer-tax system will not affect the location of the latter or the freedom of access for their products to the whole of East Africa. Doubtless, there are industries which can operate efficiently within the market of any one of the partner states, though it would require more information about economies of scale than is available to be certain that there are many which could not operate more efficiently in a larger market. What is more questionable is that there are industries which, because of their economies of scale, could operate with reasonable efficiency to serve the whole of East Africa, but which would be so inefficient if confined to the market of a single partner state that a multiplication of plants within East Africa would be impossible. In the first place, one may doubt if economies of scale are usually likely to have so convenient a 'shape'. Secondly, the assumption that there are industries which could be attracted by the availability of the whole East African market, but would not be established to serve the market of a single partner state, neglects the fact that the high costs of a small market may not always be of decisive concern to the investor, and can in any case be offset within a wide range by the provision of favourable terms, such as a very short write-off period. The President of Tanzania, in a speech to the East African Legislative Assembly, pointed out that:

> Each of the Partner States goes ahead on its own, trying to interest foreign firms or foreign governments in such a project. And the foreign firms do sometimes agree. After all, their main concern is to sell their machinery to us, either for purposes of extending their competition to East Africa, or simply as a means of making immediate profit for themselves. In either case the cost of the necessary subsidy will have to be borne by us. So we have the absurd position where both Kenya and Tanzania, in partnership with competing foreign firms, set up a tyre factory – each of which requires the whole East African market to be economic.[3]

In reality, therefore, it cannot safely be assumed that the Treaty mechanisms will prevent a multiplication of plants in which there is a very substantial loss of scale economies.

What effect the individual partner states expected the transfer-tax system to have on their economic prospects must be a matter for conjecture. It is important to remember that Kenya accepted the transfer taxes in exchange for the removal of quantitative restrictions. Although the transfer taxes would restrict inter-state trade, as compared with the actual situation at the time of the Treaty they represented a substantial liberalization.

Kenya perhaps believed that her more efficient productive environment would enable her industries to compete in the rest of East Africa over transfer taxes that could not exceed 50 per cent of the external tariff. It is probable that she had not considered the full implications of the rules governing transfer taxes. First, the tax was to be assessed on the value of the goods, so that it was to be levied on the imported content as well as on the value added in Kenya. As a result, the effective rate of protection accorded a Tanzanian or Ugandan producer was greater than that indicated by the rate of tax. Secondly, if the imported content of Kenya goods and the customs duty paid on it were high enough, they could be at a disadvantage as compared with imports from outside the common market, despite the limitation of the transfer tax to 50 per cent of the import duty on the product.[4] However, offsetting the effect of this discrimination against Kenya, and probably given more weight, was the requirement that a diversion of imports from Kenya to outside sources had to be corrected, so that it was expected that only the increased competitiveness of Tanzanian and Ugandan producers would impinge on Kenya's trade.

The rules restricting the scope of transfer taxes according to the size of the trade imbalance, and the ability of the tax-imposing country to produce the product, may also have helped persuade Kenya to accept the system. Given the fact that the domestic market for manufactures was much larger in Kenya than in the other countries, and that the transfer taxes would not affect the location of single-plant industries serving the whole East African market, Kenya may reasonably have concluded that the transfer-tax system would have no more than a moderate influence on the balance of locational advantage within East Africa.

Tanzania, on the other hand, could have suspected that this conclusion relied too heavily on the impossibility of the duplication of plants in large-scale industries. If duplication were not impossible, Tanzania could expect to establish some large-scale industries, despite the attractions of Kenya. And the possibility of duplication increased the attractiveness of a Tanzanian location, in which there would be no possibility of the products being transfer-taxed.

If Tanzania and Uganda did not expect their locational advantage for large-scale industries to be significantly increased by the transfer-tax system, they must have accepted the fact that the industries which it would foster would be industries which could successfully operate within their national markets, and which did not require the whole East African market for efficiency. Presumably, they expected that the growth of these industries within the lifetime of the transfer taxes would establish a sufficient industrial base for them to be able to compete with Kenya on an equal footing. The Treaty did not give Tanzania and Uganda the benefits they could have obtained by abandoning the preference for the goods of their common-market partners, and importing from cheaper sources outside East Africa. But such a policy would also have abandoned their prospect of developing industries to serve the wider East African market in the longer run. And under the Treaty the longer run was to be brought nearer by a new institution, the East African Development Bank.

(D) THE EAST AFRICAN DEVELOPMENT BANK

The Treaty provided for the establishment of an East African Development Bank with an initial capital of £20 million, to be subscribed mainly by the three East African countries, though provision was made for participation by other institutions. The initial subscription of the three partner states was set at £12 million, but only half was to be paid-in capital, and this was to be paid in instalments over eighteen months, so that the commitment of each country was to subscribe £2 million by 1 June 1969. The purposes of the Bank are to promote industrial development, to give priority to the relatively less industrially developed partner states, to finance projects designed to make the economies of the partner states increasingly complementary in the industrial field, and to supplement and co-operate with the national development agencies of the partner states and other institutions concerned with industrial development.

Expression is given to the 'equalizing' aim of the Bank by the requirement that only a little under a quarter of its resources should be invested in Kenya, and the remainder equally in the other two partner states. The required territorial distribution of funds is stated quite precisely in the Charter of the Bank: $38\frac{3}{4}$ per cent in Tanzania; $38\frac{3}{4}$ per cent in Uganda; $22\frac{1}{2}$ per cent in Kenya. The rigidity of so precise an allocation is relieved by the qualification that it should be achieved 'as nearly as possible' on average over consecutive five-yearly periods. Nevertheless, other arrangements might have given the Bank more elbow-room to reconcile the requirements that, on the one hand, it should favour the less-developed partner states and, on the other, it should invest only in economically sound projects.

For example, if it had been provided simply that not less than 25 per cent of the Bank's total funds should be invested in each country, each would have had a guaranteed minimum of a quarter, and the possibility of attracting up to half of the funds. Alternatively, it could have been laid down that the 'ordinary' funds of the Bank should be invested according to strict commercial criteria, uninfluenced by considerations of the territorial location of the investment, and that 'special' funds, which might have been obtained on favourable terms, should be concerned with 'equalization'. As it is, this sensible and desirable use of the idea of special funds has been lost, for it appears that the 'Special Funds' of the Bank must be invested on as strict criteria as the ordinary funds. The Charter of the Bank, on this question, seems a curious mixture of two different and not wholly compatible ideas.

The equalizing influence of the Bank's investment rule is diminished by the fact that the better investment climate of Kenya could be expected to make other funds more readily available than in the other partner states. In consequence, as much investment in total (bank funds *plus* other funds) might be achieved in bank-financed projects in Kenya, despite the smaller investment of bank funds.

The Charter makes only formal statements about the relation between the new Bank and the financial and development institutions of the individual governments and of the private sector already operating in East Africa. To supplement the activities of the national development agencies and to co-operate with other development institutions are said to be objectives of the Bank. To be successful the Bank must certainly supplement and reinforce rather than supplant the work of these other institutions. A mere diversion of funds to the new Bank which would otherwise have gone through other channels would not be an important contribution to development, though the expenditure of the funds might be different. To be successful the Bank must also be more than a passive financing institution. The need is not only for finance but also for the identification of investment opportunities. The Bank needs to be active in seeking out investment projects which will contribute to the development of East Africa. In this connection it is perhaps to be regretted that the Bank must confine itself to promoting industrial development, industry being defined to include the processing of agricultural, forestry, and fishing products, but to exclude building, transport and tourism. Some investments in infra-structure might, by stimulating directly productive investment, materially promote the equalizing function of the Bank.

An East African Development Bank could act as a fund rather than a bank, and be little more than a means of channelling money into the less-developed of the countries, not only from outside East Africa but also from the more-developed of the three, herself an extremely poor country. The Charter of the Bank, including the rules for the appointment of the Board and the officials, seems designed to prevent the development of the institution along these lines. However, if no additional funds were forthcoming, Kenya would contribute one-third of the capital and obtain less than a quarter of the investment funds. On the other hand, a sufficient inflow of funds to the Bank in addition to the capital contribution of the partner states could make the share of each partner state greater than its contribution. The Bank could then benefit all partner states as well as serving as an instrument for influencing the location of industry against the tendency for industrial development to concentrate in Kenya.

(E) COMMUNITY FINANCE

The Treaty arranged for the fiscal redistribution through the Distributable Pool to be ended. The Pool was designed as compensation for the inequitable operation of the common market and was to be replaced by new equalizing devices: the transfer taxes, and the Development Bank. The Treaty did not provide for the immediate abolition of the Pool; it was to be phased out as the new arrangements were introduced. Payments into the Pool for redistribution were to be halved when the first transfer tax was imposed, and were to come to an end a year after Kenya paid the second instalment of her capital contribution to the Bank, that is in the middle of 1969. Allowing for the way in which the Treaty provided for the finance of the non-self-contained common services, Kenya was to gain about £$\frac{1}{2}$ million, and Tanzania and Uganda to lose about £$\frac{1}{4}$ million each from the disappearance of the Pool.

Instead of the old system, in which the non-self-contained common services were allocated a fixed percentage of the revenue from certain taxes, the Treaty provided for the appropriation from the yield of those taxes the amount required to meet the expenditures. With the rise in tax yields, the fixed percentage had provided EACSO with funds too liberally for the treasuries of the partner states to be happy with the arrangement.

(F) AGRICULTURE

The Treaty deals summarily with agriculture. Article 12, paragraph 3, and Article 13 lay down that despite Article 12, paragraph 1, which prescribes the absence of quantitative restrictions on inter-state trade in East African products, including agricultural products, quantitative restrictions can be imposed on the products listed in Annex III 'which are basic staple foods or major export crops, subject to special marketing arrangements'. Article 14 says that, notwithstanding Article 12, paragraph 3, and Article 13, it is the long-term aim to extend the Common Market to agriculture and the trade in agricultural produce. Annex III lists sixteen products for which no limit is set on their liability to quantitative restrictions, one product for which the limit is three years, and nine for which it is one year.

One reason why free inter-state trade in all agricultural products could not be immediately instituted was the existence of 'artificial' price structures for some products which resulted from the operation of 'organized' marketing by statutory authorities. In Kenya most agricultural products were subject to statutory control, and in Tanzania extensive organized marketing arrangements had been introduced for a wide range of products. In Uganda marketing was relatively uncontrolled, except for the long-established marketing boards for cotton and coffee, although here also the trend was to the extension of statutory marketing. The pursuit of different price policies by the marketing agencies, or the existence of a guaranteed price in one country and a free market price in another, made it necessary to maintain the power to control inter-state trade if marketing arrangements were not to be disrupted. Not all crops could have been included in Annex III for this reason, and it seems that some were put on the list simply because of a desire to protect domestic producers. The Treaty therefore appears to pay little more than lip-service to the principle of a common market in agricultural products. The scope for beneficial co-operation in agricultural trade is discussed in Chapter 9.

(G) MONETARY ARRANGEMENTS

The provisions of the Treaty made the three currencies very close to a single currency. Restrictions on inter-state payments, such as were imposed for a brief period in the first part of 1967 subsequent to the nationalization of the banks in Tanzania, were proscribed by the Treaty, which guaranteed freedom of current transactions between the partner states without exchange charges. Currency notes were to be freely exchangeable, at a charge no greater than was required to cover the cost of transporting currency notes between the countries. Current-account transactions were not accorded freedom from control, but the control was to be exercised simply to identify genuine current-account from capital transactions, and was not to be used with restrictive intent. The Treaty's authorization of controls over intra-East African capital transactions was to be expected given the long-held view that Kenya 'drained' funds from the other countries.

The partner states committed themselves to 'endeavour to harmonize their monetary policies to the extent required for the proper functioning of the Common Market and the fulfilment of the aims of the Community', and there is a formal requirement for regular meetings of the central-bank governors. This was an essential, but rather weak commitment. The conditions of monetary unification set out in the Treaty were incompatible with the pursuit by the partner states of widely different monetary policies, so that a great deal depended on the agreement to harmonize monetary policies and for each country 'to pursue an economic policy aimed at ensuring the equilibrium of its overall balance of payments and confidence in its currency'.

The Treaty requires the central banks to settle their accounts in a currency acceptable to the creditor. It was expected that settlements would be made at frequent intervals, so that there would be no persistent net balances and consequently no significant lending between the countries. Provision is, however, separately made for a system of reciprocal credits. In certain circumstances a country in balance-of-payments difficulties can obtain credit from a partner state with which it is in deficit. The granting of these credits is hedged around with restrictions, their total amount is not over-large (on 1966 trade figures, the maximum amount Kenya would have to advance in a year would be a little over £1 million to Tanzania and £1¼ million to Uganda, and the maximum credits outstanding at any time would be £2¼ million from Kenya to Tanzania and £2½ million from Kenya to Uganda), and they were made subject to rising interest-charges over time. It is possible to visualize a system in which a surplus country in intra-East African trade had the option either of lending to its partner the amount of its surplus, or of eliminating its surplus by increasing its imports from its partner. The Treaty went only a very short way in the direction of such a payments scheme, and therefore permitted Kenya to continue to be able to earn foreign exchange from her intra-East African surplus.

(H) HARMONIZATION OF POLICIES

In addition to monetary harmonization, the Treaty deals with the harmonization of a wide range of policies of the three governments, but by declarations of intent rather than by firm commitments. These intentions refer to taxation, commercial laws, transport policies, and national planning, but no specific measures in any of these fields are set out in the Treaty.

The Treaty has more specific provisions concerning the external tariff and excise duties. The governments agreed in the Treaty to abolish differences in the external tariff and any differences in the excise tariff which would hinder the proper functioning of the common market. The differences at the time of the Treaty were not numerous. The Treaty provides for quantitative controls to be maintained where excise differences could have an adverse effect on the revenue of one of the states. It also provides for the existence of agreed differences in rates of duty, so long as they do not affect the proper operation of the common market. The Treaty can in fact be read not as prescribing a rigid standardization of rates of duty, but as providing for agreed differences. The earlier agreements on customs and excise matters did not envisage variations from the common rates, and the differences which had developed in the few years prior to the Treaty were strictly in violation of the agreements.

Although taxation in the partner states, other than import and excise duties, is left by the Treaty as a matter for the individual governments, with only a commitment in general terms to consult over the harmonization of policies, there is one aspect of taxation policy which is singled out for more particular attention. As a measure to promote balanced industrial development the partner states declared that they would 'use their best endeavours to agree upon a common scheme of fiscal incentives towards industrial development' (Article 19). Nothing is said about the nature of the scheme, but as it is an equalizing measure an appropriate scheme would presumably not standardize incentives, but would allow the less-developed partner states to offer greater incentives than the more-developed.

One of the purposes of the harmonization of policies in a common market is to support the agreement on freedom of trade between the members, and to prevent other policies from interfering with the operation of the area as a unified market. We have already noted the fact that the Treaty requires any trade deviation resulting from the imposition of transfer taxes to be corrected. It also requires deviations resulting from barter agreements between a partner state and a foreign country to be corrected. Government and Community imports are exempted from customs duties, but not if they are for re-sale to the public. Goods provided under economic-aid arrangements are not exempt from duty if they are to be transferred outside the partner state which is the recipient of the aid. No partner state may negotiate tariff concessions with a foreign country which are not available to the other partner states. Various discriminatory practices are recognized as being incompatible with the Treaty 'to the extent that they frustrate the benefits expected from the removal or absence of duties and quantitative restrictions on trade between the Partner States' (Article 16). These practices are identified as one-channel marketing, discriminatory taxation of another partner state's goods, dumping, and discriminatory purchasing of foreign goods when suitable goods are available from within East Africa at comparable prices.

Despite these various provisions, the Treaty does not fully establish a position in which there is equality in the terms of competition between the partner states in all parts of the common market, with a preference over foreign goods determined by the external tariff (as modified temporarily by transfer taxes). Deviations in a partner state's imports from another partner state to a foreign supplier as a consequence of aid agreements do not appear to be covered by any provision of the Treaty. There appears to be nothing preventing a government from discriminatory purchasing in favour of its own industries as compared with those of another partner state. It must not discriminate in favour of foreign suppliers, but the goods of the different partner states are not all to be treated equally in this respect, and a government is not precluded from supporting its own country's industries.

(I) THE COMMON SERVICES

The first thing to be said about the common services is that the Treaty provided for them all to be continued to be operated in common, except for the Aptitude Testing Unit and, by implication, the University of East Africa after 1970. But major changes were instituted by the Treaty in the self-contained services.

All the self-contained services were to be formed into public corporations, whereas before the Treaty only East African Airways had that form of organization. The new Corporations were to be under the control of boards of directors, whose terms of appointment and qualifications attempted to ensure that they would not be simply representatives of their own governments, concerned primarily with national rather than East African interests. The railways administration was to be separated from that of the harbours, and two separate corporations were to be set up. A measure of decentralization to regional headquarters was to be introduced into the administration of the services, and there were commitments to favour the less-developed partner states in the expansion of the services, some in general and others in more specific terms. Finally, it was provided that the headquarters of the self-contained services, which were all established in Nairobi, should be distributed more equally among the partner states. This was a matter on which the Philip Commission had been unable to agree, and it was settled only at the last moment before the signature of the Treaty by the Heads of State. In the re-location of headquarters, the railways and airways headquarters, which would have been the most costly to move, were to remain in Nairobi. The headquarters of the new Harbours Corporation were to be set up in Dar es Salaam, though it was recognized that Mombasa would continue to be the chief port of East Africa. The headquarters of the postal and telecommunications services were to be moved to Kampala. And Kampala was to be the seat of the East African Development Bank.

The corporations are required to conduct their business according to commercial principles, and to cover their costs taking one year with another. But a corporation is required 'to have regard to its revenues in the territories of the Partner States as a whole and not to its revenues in any particular Partner State or area within the territories of the Partner States' (Article 72.3). Cross-subsidization between the states, and within any state, was therefore still to be permitted. In fact, the existence of cross-subsidization through the self-contained services was doubtless one of the considerations that persuaded one or more of the states to accept the 'package' presented in the Treaty. Although cross-subsidization is permitted, the Treaty attempts to protect the corporations from pressure by governments to provide non-remunerative services, and the so-called 'branch-line formula', which operated in the railways, under which a government could be called upon to contribute towards the cost of a service it had requested, was extended to the other services.

The changes introduced by the Treaty in the non-self-contained or General Fund services were perhaps less radical than those in the self-contained services. The financial changes have already been discussed, and changes in the government of the services are explained below. There was to be some decentralization of administration, in the tax-collecting services for example, but the major change was the transfer in the location of the administration. The headquarters of EACSO were in Nairobi. The Community headquarters were to be set up in Arusha.

Many of the changes in the common services effected by the Treaty must be seen as additional 'equalizing' measures introduced to support those concerned with inter-state trade and industrial investment. The concentration of the expenditures of the common services in Kenya had for long been objectionable to Tanzania and Uganda. The agreement on the re-location of the headquarters, together with the establishment of the East African Development Bank, gave each partner state the head-quarters of two Community institutions, including that of the Community itself, with a consequent redistribution of their income-generating expenditures and the employment they provide in favour of Tanzania and Uganda. An attempt to measure the effects of the re-location of the services on the national incomes of the partner states led to the conclusion that the re-location provisions of the Treaty were perhaps among its most important parts, and involved an unquestioned sacrifice on the part of Kenya.[5] The decentralization was also intended as an equalizing measure, giving each partner state a closer connection with the administration of the services, and shifting some expenditures to the regions. The effect of the changes on the efficiency of the services might be in both directions. Some of the services could have been over-centralized, and the changes could make an improvement in efficiency possible. In others, decentralization, as well as the shifts in location, could be expected to be costly in terms both of money and efficiency. But it was expected that the increased costs would offset only to a relatively small extent the economies of joint operation which the Treaty preserved.

(J) THE GOVERNMENT OF THE COMMUNITY

The Treaty introduced a number of innovations into the government of the integration arrangements. The keystone of the arrangements – the Authority, composed of the three Heads of State – was retained. The Central Legislative Assembly, renamed the East African Legislative Assembly, was also retained. The size of the Assembly was reduced, it being laid down that it should consist of nine members appointed by each partner state, a chairman, the Secretary General and the Counsel to the Community, and the holders of six newly created offices – the East African Ministers and Deputy East African Ministers. The business of the Assembly as prescribed in the Treaty is to pass Bills concerning the functions of the Community (financial Bills may be introduced only by a Minister), and to receive the annual reports of the Corporations.

The office of East African Minister (and Deputy Minister) was an important innovation of the Treaty. The East African Ministers replaced the 'triumvirates' of ministers of the individual countries which controlled the common arrangements under EACSO. They have Cabinet rank in their own countries, but not national departmental responsibilities. Although it is not required by the Treaty, functional responsiblities have been allocated to the East African Ministers. One is responsible for common-market and economic-planning matters, one for finance and administration, and the third for communications, social affairs and research. Each Minister is supported by a secretariat. Although it has no sanction from the Treaty, the practice has been to allocate the main appointments under the Ministers between the partner states in such a way that, for example, the Minister and the chief officer in his secretariat are not from the same partner state.

The secretariats service the Ministerial Councils, another innovation. The Treaty established five councils: the Common Market Council; the Communications Council; the Economic Consultative and Planning Council; the Finance Council; and the Research and Social Council. The Councils are composed of the three East African Ministers and three Ministers from the government of each of the partner states, except that the partner-state Ministers on the Finance Council are limited to the three Ministers of Finance. The Treaty lays down that on the other Councils the partner states shall be represented by any three Ministers from each.

The Common Market Council is required to supervise the operation of the common-market provisions of the Treaty, and it is assisted in this function by the Common Market Secretariat, which is directed to 'keep the functioning of the Common Market under continuous examination' (Article 31). The Communications Council has specific duties concerning the control of the corporations, as well as providing a forum for consultation on communications matters. The other councils have a consultative and advisory function, though in addition the Finance Council must approve major financial decisions affecting the common services.

Decisions of the councils require unanimity. The fact that it is the partner-state Ministers who have to agree makes the Councils less of a change from the EACSO system of ministerial 'triumvirates' than might appear. If there is a failure to agree, either no progress can be made with the matter concerned, or it is referred to the Authority for a decision. With regard to common-market affairs, however, there is an additional element in the decision-making machinery, a judicial body, the Common Market Tribunal. The Tribunal can make binding decisions, by a majority vote, on matters referred to it concerning the observance and interpretation of the common-market provisions of the Treaty.

In a sense there are no sanctions for the observance of the Treaty, nor could there be, except for the ultimate sanction open to an aggrieved member of repudiating the Treaty and withdrawing from the Community. The arrangements for the government of the Community were designed to ensure as far as possible that differences between the partner states are not pursued to that point.

(K) ASSESSMENT

The conclusion of the Treaty was an act of high statesmanship by the East African countries. They withdrew from the brink of disintegration with an agreement to continue and to codify the common arrangements, and in several directions to extend them. An assessment of the Treaty at the time that it was concluded, without the benefit of a knowledge of future developments, might have welcomed the Treaty while recognizing the possibility of future difficulties and disappointments if any of the partner states expected large, obvious and rapid benefits from the changes introduced.

The advantages and disadvantages to the different partner states were very nicely balanced. Kenya gained to the extent that the alternative was a dissolution of the common market, though she lost as compared with the freedom of trade she enjoyed in the past. Kenya also lost from the changes in the common services, though probably not enough to out-weigh the economies of continued operation of the services in common. And her gains from the Bank were at best uncertain. Tanzania and Uganda benefited from the continuation of the common services and from the decision to decentralize and to re-locate headquarters, and they were likely to benefit from the operations of the Bank. They would lose the fiscal redistribution through the Distributable Pool, and they would gain little in the short run from the continuation of the common market.[6] It seemed possible that the two main innovations of the Treaty, the transfer-tax system and the Development Bank, would be note-worthy for their novelty rather than for the rapid changes they would effect in the East African economy. The currency arrangements pre-served most of the advantages of a common currency, but they would work only if the three governments were prepared to harmonize closely their monetary policies.

It seemed, therefore, that the immediate importance of the Treaty rested mainly on its demonstration of the desire for continued and ex-tended co-operation. East Africa as a whole might gain not only from the existence of the common market and common services, but also from the favourable effect on business attitudes of the fact that – after all the uncertainties and doubts of the preceding years – the three countries had signed a Treaty giving for the first time a firm legal basis to the common market and indicating the intention of the governments to maintain and reinforce the economic cohesion of East Africa.

NOTES

[1] Parts of this chapter are based on Hazlewood, A., 'The Treaty for East African Co-operation', *Standard Bank R.*, Sept. 1967.

[2] *Treaty for East African Co-operation* (Nairobi: Government Printer on behalf of the East African Common Services Organization, 1967). For comments on the Treaty see articles by Robson, P., Rothchild, D., Ghai, Y. P., Roe, A. R., Helleiner, G. K., and Hazlewood, A., *East Afr. Econ. R.*, Dec. 1967.

[3] *The Standard* (Dar es Salaam), 9 Feb. 1972.

[4] See Diamond, P. A., 'Effective Protection of the East African Transfer Taxes', *East Afr. Econ. R.*, Dec. 1968. For another application of the concept of effective protection see Pearson, S. R., and Page, J. M., 'Redistribution of Industry in the East African Common Market', *B. Oxford Univ. Inst. Econ. Statist.*, Nov. 1971.

[5] Roe, A. R., loc. cit.

[6] Roe, A. R., 'Terms of Trade and Transfer Effects in the East African Common Market: An Empirical Study', *B. Oxford Univ. Inst. Econ. Statist.*, Aug. 1969, concluded that 'in the short run, the size of Tanzania's net gain (or loss) from customs union membership is unlikely to be unduly affected by the provision of the Treaty; the short run redistributive effects of the transfer tax may just about compensate for the downgrading of the distributable pool. In the short run therefore, even if Tanzania does not actually lose from her membership of the union, she will continue as the most marginal of its members.'

8 The East African Community Since the Treaty [1]

(A) THE GOVERNMENT OF THE COMMUNITY

The institutions established by the Treaty to govern the Community appear to have worked tolerably well during the first three years of their existence. The headquarters were established in Arusha. The Common Market Council settled a number of disputes about inter-state trade, often concerning matters of minute detail, but not for that reason unimportant. Most disputes were settled by agreement, though some awaited reference to the Common Market Tribunal, which was never fully constituted. One important issue between the partner states which remained in practice unsettled, despite agreement in principle, was the effect on inter-state trade of the operation of state trading organizations (see Chapter 9).

The Treaty was applied less easily to the government of the communications services than to the control of the common market. There were, of course, greater administrative changes to be carried out, and there was, it may be suspected, some deliberate 'dragging of feet'. The division of East African Railways and Harbours into two Corporations and the re-location of the various Corporations' headquarters were delayed. The development programmes were not considered by the Communications Council at the prescribed time, but the timetable had admittedly been unrealistic. Agreement could not be reached on the purchasing of locomotives for the Railways Corporation, and Kenya began to make arrangements to purchase locomotives herself for use on her own section of the system. However, the difficulties were eventually resolved, partly by the intervention of the Authority. The division of the Railways and Harbours took place in the middle, instead of at the beginning of 1969, the Posts and Telecommunications Corporation headquarters were established in Kampala, the development plans were considered and approved, and the differences over the purchase of locomotives were patched up.

During this initial period other arrangements of the Treaty began to function. The Economic Consultative and Planning Council initiated studies of industrial co-ordination. The central bankers met regularly, and for a time free convertibility between the three currencies was maintained. Community legislation was prepared by the Secretariat and passed by the East African Legislative Assembly. The secretariats serviced the councils effectively, and they also serviced several committees of officials, such as the Committee of Planners, which did useful work. It is true that the councils met less regularly than might have been helpful, and meetings were subject to cancellation at short notice when one or other of the Ministers, from one or other of the partner states, was prevented from attending by what he thought was more urgent or important business. However, the performance of the councils was improved by a directive from the Authority, which also, as in the past, seemed able in its private sessions to solve problems its subordinates had found insoluble.

It is no criticism that the partner states, in operating the Community, put their national interests first: it was their duty to do so. The purpose of the Community is to serve the interests of the partner states so that each believes itself to be better off than if the Community did not exist. The institutions of the Community were designed to achieve an acceptable distribution of the benefits of co-operation, but it would be astonishing if they operated at all times without strains and stresses. It is proper to criticize officials and Ministers of a partner state for giving lower priority to Community matters than to their own national affairs, because Community affairs do not necessarily have less bearing on the national interest than matters within the competence of the national government. But the more immediate political impact of national matters perhaps makes the order of priority understandable. In any case, on the whole, the new Community institutions worked, and their teething troubles appeared to be coming to an end. They seemed even to be helping – in the work of the Planning Council for instance – not only to regulate but also to stimulate the process of economic integration in East Africa.

Much was changed, however, in January 1971 with the advent to power of a military régime in Uganda. The Authority did not meet after that event, and still had not met by October 1974. For some time, Tanzania refused to recognize the new régime in Uganda, she blocked Ugandan nominations to certain Community appointments, and there were clashes between the armed forces of the two partner states. After relations had been superficially restored to normal, the underlying tensions remained and came to the surface from time to time. All this had a disrupting effect on the work of the Community.

One difficulty for the Community of the rupture in relations between two of the partner states soon became apparent. The Appropriation Act for 1971, on which the normal financing of the Community depended, could not be brought into operation in the absence of the signatures of all members of the Authority. It appeared for a time that the financial base for the Community's operations would collapse. However, it so happened that the General Fund of the Community had accumulated large surplus balances, and essential payments were made and the Community kept going by drawing upon these. Later, a way was devised for obtaining the consent of the Authority to legislation without the Heads of State assembling in person, and this particular crisis was overcome.

Such devices did not return the Community to normal. Previously, the Authority had been a force for political discipline in the councils, and in the absence of Authority meetings a good deal of slackness developed. Meetings of the councils became increasingly difficult to organize, and unattended business accumulated. Studies carried out by the secretariats and commissioned from consultants failed to receive attention, so that there was no progress with the implementation of proposals. The Report of a Working Party on Fiscal Incentives was one of the casualties. The problem-solving function that the Authority had exercised so successfully in the past could not be carried out. The Community continued to run under its own momentum, but it became apparent that a driving force was lacking, and in the absence of political leadership at the highest levels not only could new initiatives in integration not become effective, but the existing machinery was in danger of running down.

Fortunately, it is possible to conclude with a reference to one encouraging feature in the government of the Community: the East African Legislative Assembly. It may be guessed that the founders of the Community, the members of the Philip Commission, did not attribute great importance to the Assembly. Its status was diminished in the new arrangements. With the then-recent failure of the attempt at federation, the Assembly did not seem likely to be an arena in which political reputations would be made, and there was no wish that it should attract attention away from national politics. To the extent that the Community was seen as a technical arrangement for co-operation on economic matters, and not as the nucleus of a future political union, the Legislative Assembly was similarly to be a technical instrument for approving Community legislation, and not an important political forum. In keeping with this view of its status is the fact that it is attended by the East African Ministers of the partner states, who are in charge of Community activities but do not have specific national responsibilities, and not by Ministers with portfolios in the national governments. Changes in the procedures of the Assembly from those of its predecessor, the old Central Legislative Assembly of EACSO, also suggest a technical, apolitical role for the EALA. Nevertheless, the Assembly has shown signs of becoming an influence of some importance within the Community. One indication is its rejection of the proposal to abolish the common administration of income taxation, though this rejection was overridden by the paramountcy of national legislation (*see below*). Other indications, which are discussed later, are the report of the Select Committee of the Assembly on East African Airways and the establishment of a committee to consider East African federation. As a pressure group for East African co-operation the Assembly has shown signs of becoming the conscience of the Community.

(B) THE GENERAL FUND SERVICES

The General Fund Services of EACSO were all continued under the Community (except for the Aptitude Testing Unit, which was disbanded, and for the contribution to the University of East Africa, the university being divided into three separate universities in the middle of 1970 but with an Inter-University Committee for East Africa established as a Community Service), but new financial arrangements were adopted. The General Fund under EACSO had received a fixed percentage of certain tax revenues without reference to the needs of the services (3 per cent of customs and excise revenue and 20 per cent of income-tax revenue from manufacturing and finance companies, minus part of the costs of collection). This arrangement was the consequence of the financing of the General Fund from the Distributable Pool of revenue. The intention of the arrangement whereby fixed percentages of revenue were paid into the Pool was to make the extent of redistribution through the Pool a function of differences in the revenues of the territories, which it was assumed were a reflection of differences in the level of development. If, for example, Kenya developed faster than the other territories, her revenues would increase in relation to theirs, and the amount redistributed from Kenya through the Pool would increase. The other effect of the scheme, perhaps unintended, was that the receipts of the General Fund were determined by the tax yields and not by the needs of the services financed from the General Fund. This 'Raisman formula', when it was introduced, gave the services a substantial increase in revenue, and throughout the existence of EACSO the General Fund was well supplied. In addition to the inflow from East African tax revenues there were large contributions, mainly from the British Government, in grants for particular services and for the 'topping-up' of salaries under the Overseas Service Aid Scheme. In 1964–5 there was a surplus of shs. 12·6m., equal to 8 per cent of the revenue.

At the time of the Philip Commission the national treasuries eyed the finances of the General Fund with some envy. During the negotiations it was agreed that, in the future, the General Fund should be supplied with cloth according to the requirements of its coat, it being no doubt the belief of the governments that their control over the Community services would be firm enough to prevent the coat from being too lavishly tailored. Under the Treaty, therefore, although the General

Fund was to be financed from the same revenue sources as before, revenue was to be supplied only to the extent needed to meet the estimated cost of the services to be financed, the control by the partner states over the estimates of expenditure being the way in which the General Fund was to be prevented from becoming too affluent at the expense of the revenues of the partner states.

As it turned out, the new financial provisions did not end the affluence of the General Fund. Delays in the delivery of equipment for such services as the Directorate of Civil Aviation and the Meteorological Department, and an inability to fill vacant posts, resulted in expenditure falling well below the estimated level, so that there were large surpluses of revenue. In 1969–70, revenue exceeded expenditure (capital and recurrent) by shs. 54m., an amount equal to 20 per cent of the revenue. In the following year, the surplus was shs. 67m., equal to 22 per cent of the year. However, the surplus in 1972–3 had been reduced to shs. 10m., and it was expected that the under-spending would then come to an end.[2] It had been agreed that any surplus balances at the end of a year were to be handed over to the partner states. It has already been remarked that there was one beneficial side-effect of the under-spending of revenue: the accumulated surpluses enabled the activities of the Community to be carried on during the hiatus in the legislative procedures of the Community in 1971.

Kenya contributes about half the total revenue of the General Fund (*see* Tables 8.1 and 8.2), and this fact has led to some feeling that Kenya

TABLE 8.1

General Fund services: location of expenditures,
source of revenues, and distribution of consumption benefits, percentages

	Kenya	Tanzania	Uganda
1964–5			
Expenditures	62	21	17
Revenues	48	28	24
Benefits	46	29	25
1971–2			
Expenditures	57	29	14
Revenues	51	29	20
Benefits	50	26	24

Sources: Hazlewood, A., 'The Territorial Incidence of the East African Common Services', *Bulletin of the Oxford University Institute of Economics and Statistics*, Aug. 1965; East African Statistical Department, *Statistical Survey of the East African Community Institutions* (Nairobi, Aug. 1972); East African Community, *Background to the Budget, 1973–74* (Arusha, 1973); Common Market and Economic Affairs Secretariat, *Review of Economic Integration Activities within the East African Community, 1973* (Arusha, May 1973); East African Statistical Department *Economic and Statistical Review*.

subsidizes the other partner states through the General Fund services. However, conclusions about cross-subsidization between the partner states cannot be based on information about their contributions to the revenues of the General Fund alone. Attention must also be given to the distribution of the benefits. The benefits are of two kinds. One consists of the indirect benefits, in terms of employment provided and demand

TABLE 8.2

Source of General Fund revenue by type of revenue and by partner state, 1971–2

			shs. m.	
	Kenya	Tanzania	Uganda	Total
Customs	45	25	14	84
Excise	23	17	14	54
Income tax	18	8	6	32
Total	86	50	34	170

NOTE: Figures exclude revenue used to meet costs of collection.

Sources: Common Market and Economic Affairs Secretariat, *Review of Economic Integration Activities within the East African Community, 1973* (Arusha, May 1973); East African Statistical Department, *Economic and Statistical Review*.

created for goods and services, which accrue to the country in which expenditure on the services is carried out. The distribution of these benefits between the partner states may be taken to be measured by the location of the expenditures. (It was, of course, the aim of the Treaty to distribute these benefits more evenly than it was believed they had been distributed when the headquarters of almost all the common institutions were in Kenya.) The data show (see Table 8.1) that the proportion of total expenditure on the General Fund services which takes place in Kenya (57 per cent in 1971–2) is greater than the proportion of General Fund revenue contributed by Kenya (51 per cent in 1971–2). The establishment of the headquarters of the Community in Tanzania transferred substantial General Fund expenditure from Kenya, but the revenue-collecting services remained in Kenya, though with some devolution to the other partner states, as did many research establishments, and such large-spending services as the Directorate of Civil Aviation and the Meteorological Department. The proportion of expenditure taking place in Kenya declined (it was estimated at 62 per cent in 1964–5), but it is not surprising that it remains at more than half the total. The fact that a higher proportion of expenditure on the services continues to take place in Kenya than the proportion she contributes of the revenue of the General Fund suggests that, on this basis of assessment, she has not much to complain about. Nevertheless, the change in the balance of the distribution of revenues and expenditures between the mid-1960s and the early 1970s was quite substantial, and to the advantage of Tanzania.

Kenya's excess of expenditure received over revenue contributed narrowed from 14 to 6 percentage points (from 62 *minus* 48 to 57 *minus* 51); the revenue gap for Tanzania of 7 percentage points disappeared (21 *minus* 28; 29 *minus* 29); for Uganda the gap remained virtually unchanged.

The second kind of benefit is the direct benefit obtained by the use or consumption of the services of the common institutions. The presumption must be – otherwise the rationale of operating the services in common disappears – that the benefits provided by an institution are used or consumed not only by the partner state in which it is located. The Industrial Research Organization, for example, although it is located in Kenya, must be presumed to provide services also for Tanzania and Uganda. But some institutions may not provide services for every partner state (Uganda does not consume the services of the Marine Fisheries Research Organization), and a common institution may not benefit each partner state equally. The consumption of the services of the common institutions (although in total equal to the total expenditure) may be distributed between the partner states unequally, and differently from both the distribution of expenditure and the source of the revenues. The fact that a partner state may directly benefit from the common institutions, that is, consume their services, to a greater or lesser extent than it contributes to their financing means that there can be cross-subsidization between the partner states through the General Fund services.

The distribution between the partner states of the consumption benefits of the services is difficult to measure, and any figures must be taken as no more than rough orders of magnitude. An estimate for the middle 1960s[3] indicated that there was cross-subsidization from Kenya to both Tanzania and Uganda, Kenya contributing more in revenue than she received in benefit and Tanzania and Uganda less. But the redistribution was small and probably within the margin of error of the estimates (*see* Table 8.1). The figures for the early 1970s suggest that both Kenya and Tanzania were contributing more than they received in benefits, whereas Uganda was receiving more in benefits than she contributed in revenue. But again the redistribution was small, and too much should not be read into the figures. It can be said that the figures provide no evidence, despite the high proportion of revenue contributed by Kenya, that she was substantially subsidizing any other partner state; they suggest that any subsidy provided by Kenya was almost certainly more than compensated for by the indirect advantages accruing to Kenya from the high proportion of expenditure on the services which took place in Kenya. In contrast, it is possible that the low level of expenditure on the services in Uganda was not fully compensated for by the amount by which Uganda's consumption of the services exceeded her contribution to their cost.

This discussion of the distribution of the benefits and costs of the

General Fund services has, as it were, treated one country's gain as another's loss. It must be emphasized that this way of looking at the matter should not be allowed to obscure the fact that all might gain from economies of scale in the operation of the services. Although cross-subsidization between the partner states is possible because of differences in the territorial distribution of revenues and benefits, all may be better off as a result of the operation of the services in common on a Community-wide basis.

A major change in the General Fund services came into effect at the beginning of 1974: the East African Income Tax Department ceased to exist, and the administration of income tax on both individuals and companies became the responsibility of the individual partner states. The rates of taxation had always been the responsibility of the individual countries; it was the assessment and collection of income tax that had been undertaken by the Community. In the past the rates of tax had been harmonized, although it had been questioned whether it was necessary to impose this particular constraint on the freedom of action of the national governments so tightly.[4] In fact, income taxation in the partner states had effectively ceased to be harmonized, and substantial differences had developed from the middle 1960s when special development taxes, which were in effect supplementary income taxes, though not administered by the East African Income Tax Department, were introduced in Tanzania and Uganda. In any case, the freedom of movement of factors of production between the partner states was sufficiently circumscribed to diminish substantially the effect of differences in the tax systems. Foreign capital, of course, is free to move, which is why the Treaty provided for the establishment of a common scheme of fiscal incentives. Nevertheless, it may be wondered whether the 'nationalization' of the income-tax administration in itself significantly diminished the economic integration of East Africa. Differences in tax rates could certainly create difficulties for the employment of Community staff anywhere within the Community, whatever their national status, but this problem had to some extent been overcome by an agreement that, for example, Kenyans working for the Community in Tanzania should pay tax at the rates in force in Kenya. The dissolution of the Department created additional administrative costs. For example, residents of Tanzania had to obtain a Tax Clearance Certificate before travelling to another partner state, whereas in the past tax clearance was required only for travel outside East Africa. Nevertheless, it was the abandonment of tax harmonization rather than the dissolution of the common administration that should be seen as a significant step away from integration, but whether it was a particularly harmful step is a matter on which there can be more than one view. It must be said, however, that what might be termed the psychological effect of the dissolution, the creation of a feeling that it was only a step in a continuing process, could be harmful to confidence in the future of the Community.

The dissolution of the East African Income Tax Department made necessary a change in the arrangements for financing the General Fund. The revenue from income tax could no longer be drawn upon in the way prescribed by the Treaty. A temporary scheme was agreed upon, in which an amount equal to that contributed by income tax on average over the previous four years was to be taken from customs and excise revenues in addition to the normal contribution from those sources. In any permanent scheme, the revenue would also have to come from customs and excise, because they were the only revenue sources remaining under the administration of the Community. But on what principles should the deductions be made? Agreement was difficult because the system adopted would determine the relative contributions of the partner states. For instance, a simple exclusion of income tax and the application of the Treaty arrangements to customs and excise alone would substantially favour Kenya, because Kenya contributed a higher proportion of income tax than of customs and excise revenues. If such an arrangement had operated in 1971–2, the source of revenue would have been changed in the following way:

Contribution by partner states, shs. m.	Kenya	Tanzania	Uganda
(a) Actual	86	50	34
(b) Under Treaty system excluding income tax	81	50	39
(c) Difference	−5	..	+5

(C) THE CORPORATIONS

A large part of the transport and communications services in East Africa is operated by the corporations of the Community. The corporations are among the largest business enterprises in East Africa, and together they provide a significant part of total activity within the monetary economy, and of total wage-employment. In 1970 they contributed nearly 8 per cent of the gross domestic product of non-agricultural enterprises in the monetary economy, and 35 per cent of that of the 'transport, storage, and communications' sector. The Community contributed 6 per cent of total capital formation, 95 per cent of it being carried out by the corporations. About 5 per cent of total employment in East Africa was in Community service, nearly 90 per cent of it being with the corporations.

Despite the shift in the location of the headquarters of two of the corporations as a result of the Treaty, and the decentralization measures adopted, the bulk of the activities of all the corporations remained in Kenya. The headquarters of the Harbours Corporation was established in Dar es Salaam, but Mombasa remained the largest port. The activities of the Posts and Telecommunications administration remained on a larger scale in Kenya, despite the removal of the headquarters to Kampala. In general the shifts in the activities of the corporations after the Treaty, whether measured by revenue, expenditure, or employment, were relatively small, though not insignificant. The facts are summarized in Tables 8.3–8.5.

The new East African Railways Corporation inherited not only the railway assets and liabilities but also the problems of the old East African Railways and Harbours administration, and these were soon intensified. Competition from road haulage had for long been a problem for the railways.[5] It had been kept in check by restrictive licensing and by the high costs of operating on bad roads. Soon after the Corporation succeeded to the business, both checks on the competitiveness of road

TABLE 8.3

Distribution of employment in corporations

	Percentages						Thousands	
	Kenya		Tanzania		Uganda		East Africa	
	1967	1971	1967	1971	1967	1971	1967	1971
Railways*	n.a.	55	n.a.	33	n.a.	12	40·6	43·8
Harbours*	n.a.	56	n.a.	44	n.a.	—	2·4	5·1
Airways	n.a.	75	n.a.	15	n.a.	10	3·7	5·0
P. & T.†	59	45	24	26	17	30	8·4	10·4

*1968
†1970

NOTE: Harbours, 1971 Headquarters 6 per cent of total employment. P. & T., Headquarters employment 15 per cent of total 1967, 11 per cent 1970.

Source: Common Market and Economic Affairs Secretariat, op. cit.

TABLE 8.4

Location of expenditure by corporations

	Percentages						shs. m.	
	Kenya		Tanzania		Uganda		East Africa	
	1967	1970	1967	1970	1967	1970	1967	1970
Railways	65	67	26	25	9	8	371	420
Harbours	63	55	37	45	—	—	169	200
P. & T.	54	54	26	19	20	27	154	218
Airways	82	75	10	13	8	12	135	194

NOTE: 'Working' or 'operating' expenditure, excluding capital charges. Airways expenditure outside East Africa excluded.

Source: Common Market and Economic Affairs Secretariat, op. cit.

TABLE 8.5

Source of revenue of corporations

	Percentages						shs. m.	
	Kenya		Tanzania		Uganda		East Africa	
	1967	1970	1967	1970	1967	1970	1967	1970
Railways	66	64	25	28	9	8	521	574
Harbours	62	59	38	41	—	—	235	286
P. & T.	55	55	24	19	21	26	189	272

Source: Common Market and Economic Affairs Secretariat, op. cit.

haulage were substantially weakened. The traffic from Mombasa to Nairobi, particularly the bulk haul traffic in petroleum products, was of great importance to the economy of the railways. The railways were sufficiently low-cost carriers of petroleum products that, with road transport constrained by licensing and the state of the Mombasa–Nairobi road, it was possible to make large profits on this traffic to offset losses on other traffics. The charges made by the railways could not be varied at will by the administration but were controlled by an elaborate and lengthy procedure which made it difficult to act competitively, lowering charges where road competition was greatest. Controls over the railway tariff were continued after the Treaty, under which the consent of the Communications Council was required to any but minor alterations in the tariff. It was not easily or speedily obtained.

In 1968 the new road between Nairobi and Mombasa, with a tarmac surface, was completed, substantially reducing the costs imposed on transport operators by the condition of the road. At about the same time the practice of the Kenya transport licensing authority was changed, and licences for operating on the new road were given much more freely. An extensive road haulage of petroleum products soon developed, and a large volume of heavy vehicles travelled on the road. The design and construction standards of the road were inadequate for this traffic; the road surface began to disintegrate and accidents proliferated.

A second effect of the expansion of road transport was a diversion of high-rated traffics from the railway. Although the volume of traffic carried and total revenue continued to rise, the revenue per unit of traffic declined, and the railways became increasingly unprofitable. Although the constraints on alterations in the railway tariff made it possible to go only a small way, and with considerable delay, towards meeting the increased competition by tariff changes, reduced charges for petroleum products were introduced in April 1969. In 1970 there was a sharp rise in the carriage of petroleum products by rail, the effect of the reduction in charges being supplemented by the carriage of supplies of oil for the Tanzania–Zambia railway construction. But the reduction in charges diminished the profitability of petroleum traffic and adversely affected the general financial position of the railways at a time when large debts had to be serviced and there were heavy depreciation charges on new equipment. A surplus of shs. 3m. in 1966 had become a deficit of shs. 8m. in 1967, which had increased to shs. 26m. in 1970.[6]

The railways were assisted in their competition with road transport by the imposition of axle-load restrictions on road vehicles by the Kenya Ministry of Works when the effect of the heavy traffic on the Mombasa–Nairobi road was seen. However, this restraint on road transport was not enforced for long. It was objected that the restrictions were hindering the development of African businessmen (there had been much investment in vehicles by well-placed Kenyans), and they were relaxed. The underlying financial weakness of the Corporation continued.

The difficulties of the Corporation reached crisis dimensions towards the end of 1973, when its future as a Community service was thrown in doubt. A speech by a Tanzanian Minister created the impression that Tanzania was about to take over the operation of her own railway system. That Tanzania had made such a decision was not implausible, for it could have been stimulated by a belief that the Tanzanian part of the system was subsidizing the remainder. It had usually been the opinion that there was the reverse pattern of subsidization: the heavy traffic on the Kenya–Uganda line subsidizing the more extensive and less intensively used Tanzanian system. There are some grounds for thinking that there might have been a change in the pattern of cross-subsidization. The economic difficulties of Uganda, and Kenya's import restrictions, reduced traffic on the Kenya–Uganda line; the construction work on the Tanzania–Zambia Railway, and Zambia's policy of diverting traffic from her southern outlets, provided additional traffic over part of the Corporation's system in Tanzania. It is also possible that Tanzania believed the Kenya Government to be allowing excessive road competition, as it was more concerned with the interests of the road-haulage industry than with those of the railway, the losses of which after all were borne only partly by Kenya.

The rumours that Tanzania was to withdraw from the Corporation coincided with a hold-up in the transfer of revenue from Tanzania and Uganda to the Kenya headquarters of the Corporation, perhaps partly for reasons connected with foreign-exchange control. The consequence was that the banks refused to honour cheques drawn on the Corporation's account, the staff at headquarters could not be paid, and the Railways Training School was closed.

After a time the Kenya Government decided to intervene to secure the payment of the staff and the reopening of the School. (There was also retaliation in the form of a failure to transfer revenues from Mombasa to the headquarters of the Harbours Corporation in Dar es Salaam.) Early in 1974 the whole question was examined by the

Communications Council and the rift between the partner states was said to have been bridged. By March 1974 it was reported that the situation in the Railways Corporation had returned to normal. At the same time, however, perhaps anticipating the findings of a Select Committee of the Legislative Assembly that had been examining the Corporation, the press was alleging the existence of large-scale corruption and dishonesty in the administration of the railways' affairs.

Within a few months of the apparent settlement of the differences between the partner states over the railways, the same problem recurred. Funds were not being transferred between the partner states. There were strikes by railway workers in June and July over the delayed payment of wages. The Select Committee report appeared in June, with allegations of gross mismanagement and dishonesty. Expenditure on fuel had quadrupled, and the financial state of the Corporation had by this time become so bad that it could not buy enough spare parts to keep its services fully in operation. The railway-tariff question was now not one of nice adjustments in its structure, but of raising charges in general to a remunerative level. The delay in authorizing tariff changes had been such that, with the rise in costs, the new tariff was already out of date when it was introduced at the beginning of May. However, an additional levy estimated to increase revenue by shs. 100m. a year was approved later in that month, and approval was given in September for further changes in the level and structure of the tariff.

At the end of July other steps were taken to deal with the situation. At a meeting of the Finance Council it was agreed that transfers of funds should be resumed, and that the partner states should make loans to the Corporation totalling £7·5m. Meetings took place with the World Bank, and it was reported that consultants were to be appointed to devise a regionalization programme. In reply to rumours that the Corporation was to be split up, it was said that there was to be 'a delegation of operational powers'. It seemed that, if the Corporation was not to be dissolved, at least there would be a very wide degree of decentralization.

East African Airways, not long after the Treaty came into force, committed a major commercial error in embarking on an unprofitable expansion of its services. Services to the Far East and the United States were inaugurated and later withdrawn when it became clear that the losses could not be borne. This error was, however, only one element in the financial difficulties of East African Airways, the magnitude of which is indicated by the fact that, despite constantly increasing revenue, a net operating surplus of shs. 14·3m. in 1968 had become a deficit of shs. 60·8m. in 1971.

It is one of the more optimistic features of the working of the Community institutions that a Select Committee of the Legislative Assembly produced a report on East African Airways in 1973 which exposed with great frankness the deficiencies of the organization, and which stimulated the introduction of reforms.[7] Particularly important among the deficiencies uncovered was a lack of proper concern for the control of expenditure and the collection of revenue. On one occasion it was discovered that coupons from other airlines worth shs. 2m. had been thrown into a dustbin at the Corporation's headquarters. Uncollected debts amounted to 37 per cent of revenue in 1970. The effects of dishonesty and incompetence were added to the difficulties created by a shortage of capital, which had led to large and expensive borrowing. Interest charges had risen from 1 per cent of revenue in 1960 to over 5 per cent in 1971. In 1972 the partner states had agreed to increase their capital contribution to the Corporation by a total of shs. 69m., but nothing had in fact been paid.

The report dealt with two questions bearing on important matters of principle. It drew attention to the large losses on the domestic routes, which amounted to shs. 5·1m. in 1965, shs. 10·6m. in 1967, and shs. 9·2m. in 1970. The Committee argued that most domestic routes would still make losses even if there were an increase in fares of as much as 20 per cent, and argued that unprofitable routes should be closed down unless a partner state was prepared to subsidize them. It pointed out that Tanzania had the greatest number of towns served by the Airways.

Another matter of principle concerned the management structure of the Corporation. It was clear to the Committee that the management structure had not worked properly. There were doubts as to whether the Board was composed of persons properly qualified under the requirements of the Treaty; the Council had dealt with matters that should have been decided by the Board; the Corporation had not submitted to the Council adequate development plans and annual programmes; overdrafts had been obtained in excess of the Corporation's borrowing powers without the sanction of the Communications Council; the Board had not exerted itself on matters of policy and finance, but had intervened in the day-to-day running of the Corporation. Nevertheless, the Committee believed that the Treaty and the East African Airways Corporation Act were not in principle unworkable; those concerned simply had not adhered to the rules.

Some time after the Select Committee had reported there were changes of personnel at the highest levels of the administration, and arrangements were made for a foreign airline to provide technical and managerial assistance. The partner states finally contributed shs. 61·4m. of new capital. By early 1974 the financial position of the Corporation had taken a turn for the better.

The problems with which the corporations have had to contend are in part peculiar to the services of each particular corporation. There are also more general problems arising from the organizational and governmental structure of the corporations. It is not obvious that the substitution of corporations for the administrative structure of the former 'self-contained services' of EACSO, with the addition of a Board of Directors and a Chairman of the Board to the layers of administration, has done anything for the efficiency of the services or for their accountability to the public.

It is possible that the idea of establishing the former self-contained services as corporations appealed at the time of the Philip Commission to different partner states for different, and perhaps incompatible reasons. One partner state perhaps expected that its representation on the Board of Directors would ensure that its particular national interests were given more attention in the policies of the administration than in the past; another partner state perhaps hoped (because it would best serve its own national interest) that the corporations would be more single-minded than the old administrations in their pursuit of narrowly commercial ends. It may be that both expectations have been disappointed, though there is more evidence for the former result, particularly when the role of the Communications Council is taken into account, than for the latter. There is little evidence that the insertion of the Directors between the administration and the Ministers has instilled more businesslike attitudes in the management of the services. On the other hand, Tanzania's evident dissatisfaction with the Railways Corporation suggests that she does not think the policies of the Corporation are as susceptible to her influence as she might wish. Nevertheless, there is plenty of evidence to indicate that narrowly commercial considerations are not always paramount. Purely commercial considerations cannot have determined the decision to route coffee from Western Tanzania over railway routes entirely within Tanzania to a Tanzanian harbour, instead of by what had been the usual, more direct route through Kenya to Mombasa. Nor can they be responsible for the long delays in making decisions on proposals for changes in either the structure or the level of the tariffs of the corporations.

Delays in the holding of meetings and the reaching of decisions can be more than an irritant; they can have a major effect on the viability of an institution. At a time when the finances of the railways were being ground between rising costs and a rigid tariff, proposals for tariff changes were delayed for at least eighteen months. It may be suspected that delays have resulted not only from the inherent difficulty of reaching compromise decisions, and from a low priority given to Community affairs, but also from their deliberate use when a country was not getting its own way. A change in attitudes is necessary to deal with the more general problem. So far as delays in authorizing tariff changes and approving investment programmes for the corporations are concerned, an improvement could be effected if a corporation were allowed to implement a proposal at a given time after its submission to the Council, unless an explicit directive to the contrary had been issued by the Council or by the Authority.

Another consequence of the system of government of the corporations is the tendency for extension of the services beyond what would be indicated by commercial considerations. The so-called 'branch-line formula', under which a corporation may 'refuse to provide a new service . . . at a . . . charge which is insufficient to meet the costs . . . unless the Partner State undertakes to make good the amount of the loss',[8] has proved an ineffective defence against pressure for such expansion. Projects can be presented in such a way that they are not for 'new' services, and are therefore excluded from the application of the rule. And it is politically impossible for the management to apply the rule. In pressing for extensions of the service provided within its boundaries, a partner state no doubt takes account of the fact that the cost is borne not by itself alone, but by the Community as a whole, and such pressures may not be strongly resisted by the other partner states, because they think that to do so might raise opposition to their own favourite schemes for development.[9] Nevertheless, the adverse effects of this 'project escalation' on the finances of the Corporation could be serious. It might be expected that the Ministers of Finance would be more sensitive than the Transport Ministers to the dangers of excessive expansion, and it would be beneficial if their influence were brought to bear on the decisions of the Communications Council. In 1974 there were signs that this was happening.

The disadvantages of 'project escalation' are enhanced by the fact that Community decisions cannot be taken after consideration of the full range of possibilities. An investment in crop storage might make an investment in the expansion of railway capacity unnecessary, but the Communications Council could consider only the railway investment, and not whether the investment in crop storage would be preferable. The Council could not even consider an alternative transport investment, if it were a road, because road investment is a matter for the national governments.

The compartmentalization of decision-making also affects the smooth working of the Community by encouraging each partner state to seek its maximum advantage in each sphere of activity, rather than to look for a balance of advantage from the whole. The Treaty was essentially a 'package deal' containing for each partner state both more and less desirable items, the latter being accepted as the price of the former. The same approach is desirable in the day-to-day work of the Community, and might be easier to adopt if a single Council dealt with the whole range of Community affairs. The difficulty arising from the existence of different Councils should not be exaggerated, because their memberships overlap, but it is probable that the division of responsibility reduces readiness to compromise.[10]

It can be argued with some force that broader considerations than the commercial success of the services should influence policy. Economic development in East Africa is in many ways so dependent on the services provided by the corporations that the provision of the services should not be constrained by narrow financial requirements. That may be so, but the present arrangements, despite efforts by the Secretariat to establish guide-lines, do not provide any careful or explicit assessment of what services are justified and what are not justified by such considerations. Nor do they provide for subsidies to be available from public funds. Under these circumstances the efficiency of the administration of the services will be undermined, dissatisfaction with the services will increase, and a belief will develop (rightly or wrongly) that a partner state would do better to withdraw from the Corporation and to provide the service by its own national administration.

It is, indeed, possible that a service could be better provided by a partner state for itself. The economies of joint operation, though they exist, are potential and not limitless. An efficiently run national administration might provide a better and cheaper service than a Community administration in which the potential economies of scale were swamped by inefficiency and by pressures for the provision of unprofitable services. It seems likely, despite the Tanzanian hint that she was withdrawing from the Railways Corporation, that there is still a general desire to make the corporations work, and that radical decentralization, which nevertheless retains at least some economies of joint operation, will prove an acceptable alternative to dissolution. It is perhaps relevant that the Posts and Telecommunications Corporation, in which there has been a greater degree of devolution than in the other corporations, appears to have had fewer problems and has been financially successful – its net revenue surplus increased from shs. 34m. in 1971 to shs. 60m. in 1972. But the continuation of the common services will remain uncertain unless the partner states restrain themselves from pressing what seem to be their short-term interests at the expense of the efficiency and viability of the corporations. If the common provision of transport and communications did come to an end a very large part of the edifice of co-operation would be demolished.

(D) THE EAST AFRICAN DEVELOPMENT BANK

The East African Development Bank was one of the two new 'equalizing' devices introduced by the Treaty. Its Charter directs the Bank to invest more of its funds in each of the two less-developed partner states than in Kenya, although each state subscribes equally to its equity. If the Bank invested only the equity subscribed by the partner states, it would be simply redistributive, removing funds from Kenya for investment in Tanzania and Uganda. But if it attracted sufficient additional funds its investment in Kenya would be able under the rules to exceed Kenya's subscription, so that all partner states would get in investment more than they subscribed. It would also be possible for the discriminatory effect of the investment distribution rules to be offset if the EADB component in the finance of projects were smaller in Kenya than in the other partner states (the EADB normally provides only part of the finance for a project). If, so to speak, the 'gearing' were greater for Kenya projects (and the better 'investment climate' of Kenya makes this a possibility) the smaller Bank investment could be associated with a larger total investment in Bank-assisted projects in Kenya than in the other partner states.

There are no data by which to judge whether or not Kenya has succeeded in attracting more outside funds than the other partner states for a given Bank investment. There was some evidence in the early days of the Bank's operations that this was so, but the evidence was not at all conclusive. Until more data are made available, therefore, it must be considered only as a possibility, a possibility which in any case is subject to the consideration that it cannot be assumed that the participation of the Bank is in fact in any way responsible for attracting other funds to a project.

It is possible, however, to determine what funds additional to the subscriptions of the partner states have accrued to the Bank. The subscriptions of the partner states were set at shs. 120m., the total amount to be paid in four instalments by the middle of 1969. The Bank was required to call up only part of its capital if it was unable to make use of the funds. The full subscription was in fact completed during 1970, though the disbursement of the funds had still only reached three-quarters of the total more than two years later.

In addition to the partner states' equity, a further shs. 9m. had been taken up by the end of 1970 by six foreign banks, and this amount had not increased by 1973. So far as equity capital is concerned, therefore, few additional funds had been attracted. However, the Bank was success-ful in negotiating loans from international and foreign institutions, and by the end of 1972 lines of credit were available from the World Bank, the African Development Bank and the Swedish International Develop-ment Authority totalling shs. 109m. In addition, other loans for smaller amounts, including loans for the establishment of the Bank's head-quarters in Kampala, had been raised.

The major funds available for investment amounted at the beginning of 1973 to shs. 238m., shs. 129m. of equity capital, and shs. 109m. from the lines of credit. Kenya's share of the expenditure of this total, 22·5 per cent under the Treaty rules, amounts to shs. 53·55m., which is in excess of her subscription of shs. 40m., so that all partner states should receive investments significantly in excess of their subscriptions from the funds available early in 1973. Any further funds attracted to the Bank would, of course, further increase the excess of investment carried out in each partner state over its subscription. Although by early 1973 the funds had become available for each partner state to receive more in investment than it had subscribed, they had not been fully disbursed. The situation for each of the partner states is shown in Table 8.6.

At the time of the foundation of the Bank it was not unreasonable to wonder whether it would be practicable within a relatively short period for the proportional allocation of investment prescribed by the Treaty to be achieved. It was reasonable to expect that the opportunities for investment of an appropriate quality would be greater in Kenya than in the other partner states, so that the prescribed proportions could be achieved only by delaying investments in Kenya or by embarking on investments of a lower quality in the other partner states.

TABLE 8.6

East African Development Bank: allocation of funds, February 1973

	shs. m.		
	Kenya	Tanzania	Uganda
Share of investment funds available	53·6	92·2	92·2
Contribution to equity	40·0	40·0	40·0
Approved investments	45·9	80·7	83·7
Disbursed funds	32·7	40·0	17·5

Source: East African Development Bank, *Annual Reports.*

In the first year or two of the Bank's operations the distribution of investments certainly favoured Kenya. However, by the end of its first five years the prescribed proportions had been pretty closely approached. It is true that far less than the total funds available had been disbursed, but the rate of expenditure seems to reflect the time required to plan and execute industrial investment projects rather than any deliberate restraint in order to keep down the proportion spent in Kenya (*see* Table 8.7). At

TABLE 8.7

East African Development Bank:
distribution of approved and disbursed investment funds

	Percentages					
	31.12.70		31.12.71		28.2.73	
	Approved	Disbursed	Approved	Disbursed	Approved	Disbursed
Kenya	40	53	39	41	22	36
Tanzania	42	12	44	35	38	44
Uganda	18	35	17	24	40	20
Total shs. m.	76·2	21·2	90·4	58·1	210·3	90·2

Source: East African Development Bank, op. cit.

the time when the lines of credit from the three institutions were negotiated, the Bank pointed out that the total sum represented no more than a year's commitments at the rate then achieved. It therefore seems, against some expectations, that the work of the Bank is more likely to be restricted by a shortage of funds than by a shortage of projects.

The apparent availability of sound projects is perhaps partly the consequence of the effort devoted by the Bank at the beginning of its existence to identify and develop opportunities for industrial investment. It was essential, if the Bank was to contribute seriously to development, that it should actively seek out projects and assist in their formulation. It would achieve little if it simply waited for appropriate projects to be presented to it.

On the evidence surveyed the Bank must be seen as a success. It has achieved its prescribed distribution of investments. It has also achieved a high rate of expenditure, which is a less easy task than might appear, because it cannot undertake 'infra-structure' investments, with their vast appetite for finance, and it must confine itself to 'economically sound projects'. The quality of the investments undertaken cannot be judged from the available information, and it is, of course, possible that an analysis of some projects would produce a less optimistic conclusion.

It must also be remembered that the developmental effect of the Bank's operations depends on its increasing the total of investment within East Africa and on improving the quality of the investment. If it served merely to divert funds that would otherwise have been channelled through other institutions into investments that would have been carried out by other institutions, it would not have achieved much. It is not possible to make any judgement on these issues. The fact that 'the Bank's role as a channel for development finance in East Africa is now beginning to take shape'[11] does not wholly settle the matter. Nor does the fact that the EADB 'works closely with the national development agencies of the Partner States'. It certainly cannot be assumed that the projects in which the Bank has participated would not have been carried out in the absence of such participation, or that the availability of Bank funds attracted other funds to a project. A study of the investment decision for each project would be necessary to determine what role was, in fact, played by the availability of EADB funds. A 1974 assessment of the Bank came to the conclusion that 'its role in industrial financing in East Africa will be just marginal during the next five years'.[12]

An objective of the Bank stated in its Charter is to further the aims of the Community by financing 'projects designed to make the economies of the Partner States increasingly complementary in the industrial field'. The three largest investments approved in 1972 in each of the partner states are the following: in Kenya, a loan to the Industrial and Commercial Development Corporation, the expansion of production of woollen fabrics, and the establishment of a sewing thread factory; in Tanzania, the expansion of sugar production, of aluminium-rolling facilities, and of oil-refining capacity; in Uganda, the establishment of a plywood factory and a tannery, and the expansion of cement production. All these may be admirable projects, but it is not clear in what way, in themselves, they are likely to make the partner states more complementary. They could perhaps do so if agreements existed between the partner states on a pattern of production specialization into which these, and other Bank-supported projects, would fit, but such agreements have not been concluded and face considerable obstacles (see Chapter 9).

(E) INTER-STATE TRADE
IN GOODS OF EAST AFRICAN ORIGIN[13]

Balance in inter-state trade does not feature in the Treaty as an explicit objective. Yet the rules governing the transfer-tax system are expressed in terms of various balances in inter-state trade, and public discussion in the period before the appointment of the Philip Commission, as well as the discussions of the Commission itself, paid much attention to such balances. To foster trade between the partner states is, of course, the purpose of the common market. The progress of inter-state trade must therefore be of great interest in any examination of East African economic integration since the 1967 Treaty. Particular interest attaches to the course of inter-state trade in manufactures, because the transfer-tax rules relate to trade in manufactures, not to inter-state trade as a whole, and also because they account for the bulk of inter-state trade (82 per cent in 1973).

Table 8.8 shows the main flows of inter-state trade in local manufactures, and the balance of trade, in 1967 and two post-Treaty years. The value of inter-state trade in manufactures of East African origin as a whole (the sum of such exports from the three partner states) was 24 per cent greater in 1973 than in 1967. In 1967 it had been at the same level as in 1964. Although for the Community as a whole inter-state trade in manufactures increased substantially in the six years after the Treaty, the experience of the three partner states differed. Kenya's exports to the rest of East Africa increased by shs. 231m., as compared with an increase of shs. 63m. for Tanzania, and a decline of shs. 129m. for Uganda. There are special circumstances affecting Uganda's inter-state exports, and no judgement about the effects of the Treaty and the operation of the common market can be based on the statistics of Uganda's inter-state trade after 1970. The reported persistence of large-scale smuggling of goods into Uganda in that period also makes it unwise to give too much significance to any of the statistics of Uganda's recorded trade. Tanzania's increase in exports within the common market was much smaller in absolute terms than Kenya's, but because of the low level of her exports in 1967 the proportional increase was much larger. Kenya's exports of domestic manufactures to the other partner states were about half as big again in 1973 as in 1967; Tanzania's had more than doubled between those two years.

In absolute terms the imbalances in inter-state trade in manufactures were greater in 1973 than in 1967. Kenya's surplus and Tanzania's and

TABLE 8.8

Inter-state trade in manufactures

	shs. m.		
(a) *Value of trade*	1967	1970	1973
Kenya to Tanzania	191	268	304
Kenya to Uganda	248	281	366
Kenya to Tanzania and Uganda	439	549	670
Tanzania to Kenya	42	63	99
Tanzania to Uganda	10	22	16
Tanzania to Kenya and Uganda	52	85	115
Uganda to Kenya	159	165	68
Uganda to Tanzania	40	33	2
Uganda to Kenya and Tanzania	199	198	70
Kenya from Tanzania	42	63	99
Kenya from Uganda	159	165	68
Kenya from Tanzania and Uganda	201	228	167
Tanzania from Kenya	191	268	304
Tanzania from Uganda	40	33	2
Tanzania from Kenya and Uganda	231	301	306
Uganda from Kenya	248	281	366
Uganda from Tanzania	10	22	16
Uganda from Kenya and Tanzania	258	303	382
(b) *Balance of trade*			
Kenya with Tanzania	+149	+205	+205
Kenya with Uganda	+89	+116	+298
Tanzania with Uganda	−30	−11	+14
Kenya with Tanzania and Uganda	+238	+321	+503
Tanzania with Kenya and Uganda	−179	−216	−191
Uganda with Kenya and Tanzania	−59	−105	−312

Source: *Annual Trade Reports.*

Uganda's deficits were all larger in the latter than in the former year. Tanzania's deficit, however, was only marginally larger; the increase in her deficit with Kenya having been to some extent offset by a change from a deficit to a small surplus with Uganda. Kenya's greatly increased surplus resulted from a large rise in transfers to Uganda accompanied by an almost equal decline in transfers from Uganda. Using the Treaty criterion of 'balance', Tanzania moved nearer to balance in inter-state trade in manufactures, and Uganda became much less balanced (*see* Table 8.9). The smuggling of goods into Uganda suggests that Uganda's inter-state trade may in fact be even more unbalanced than the statistics of recorded trade indicate.

Despite the growth in inter-state trade, the importance of imports of East African manufactures in relation to imports from outside East Africa declined for both Kenya and Tanzania. For both Kenya and

TABLE 8.9

Degree of balance in inter-state trade in manufactures:
exports to other partner states as percentage of imports from other partner states

	1960	1967	1970	1973
Tanzania	11	22	28	38
Uganda	93	77	65	18

Source: *Annual Trade Reports.*

Tanzania, imports from the rest of East Africa were a smaller proportion of total imports of manufactures in 1973 than in 1967, or even than in 1960. In Uganda, in contrast, the share of East African goods was higher in 1973 than in earlier years (*see* Table 8.10).

An indication of progress in the common market might be an increasing proportion of imports coming from the other partner states. The figures for Kenya and Tanzania show that the common market has not been successful in this sense. In fact, the figures are consistent with a pattern of development in which domestic production in these states was substituted for the products of the other partner states rather than for

TABLE 8.10

Imports from other partner states as proportion of total imports of manufactures

Percentages				
	1960	1967	1970	1973
Kenya	6·4	9·2	7·9	4·1
Tanzania	18·2	15·8	14·1	9·3
Uganda	19·0	25·8	27·7	37·1

Source: *Annual Trade Reports.*

imports from outside East Africa. There is no simple explanation of the relative changes in imports from outside East Africa and from the other partner states. One marked change in the import pattern of Tanzania, which must have some bearing on the matter, is the large increase in the importance of China as a source of supplies since 1969. In that year China supplied less than 5 per cent of Tanzania's total imports (i.e., from outside and from inside East Africa, manufactured and non-manufactured); by 1973 the proportion had risen to over 20 per cent (for both Kenya and Uganda it was less than 1 per cent). Over the same period, Tanzania's imports from the partner states had fallen from 17 to less than 10 per cent. Part of the increase in imports from China seems certain to have been at the expense of goods from the rest of East Africa, as perhaps in the products listed in Table 8.11, Tanzania's imports of which from Kenya declined between 1969 and 1973 and from

China increased. A good part of the imports from China come in under a commodity credit agreement for financing local costs of the Tanzania–Zambia railway, and it is not clear whether the high level of imports from China will continue after this arrangement comes to an end. Some Chinese goods are highly price-competitive, and may for that reason continue to be imported in preference to goods from Kenya. The trade-diversion provisions of the Treaty would not apply to such imports if they were cheap enough to compete whether or not Kenya goods were transfer-taxed, for in that case the diversion would not have been caused by the imposition of the tax. A long-term shift in the pattern of Tanzanian trade may, therefore, have resulted from what was initially part of the agreement on the Tanzania–Zambia railway.

TABLE 8.11

Source of Tanzania's imports of certain products, 1969 and 1973

shs. m.

	China		Kenya	
	1969	1973	1969	1973
Dentifrices	—	8·6	3·2	0·1
Toilet soap	—	10·1	9·2	2·0
Detergents	—	9·2	8·2	—
Cement	1·3	14·2	14·1	2·5
Shirts	—	4·6	1·6	0·1

Source: *Annual Trade Reports.*

There may be other, less dramatic cases where the availability of tied credits has influenced the pattern of imports of the partner states and reduced the importance of imports from within the Community. More fundamentally, however, the expansion of inter-state trade has been limited by the failure of the East African economies to develop complementary patterns of production, oriented towards a Community market. The mechanisms of the Treaty have not been strong enough to secure such developments.

Inter-state trade has also, in general, declined in importance as an outlet for the exports of the partner states. Although its relative importance has increased for Tanzania, for Kenya and Uganda exports to other partner states were a smaller proportion of total exports (to the other partner states and to the rest of the world) in 1973 than before the Treaty (*see* Table 8.12). The same pattern applies to exports of manufactures. In 1967 Tanzania and Uganda took three-quarters of Kenya's exports of the main manufactured products (SITC Sections 6, 7 and 8). In 1973 the proportion had fallen to 57 per cent. Over the same period the rest of East Africa declined in importance as an outlet for Uganda's exports of these products from 47 per cent to 30 per cent. In contrast, for

Tanzania the other partner states became relatively more important as a market for her manufactured exports, the proportion rising from 10 per cent to 21 per cent.

Even before the political changes of 1971, Uganda's performance in inter-state trade was disappointing. Uganda's inter-state exports of manufactures declined from 1967 until 1969, and recovered in 1970 to no more than their 1967 level. After 1970 the value of transfers to other partner states declined, particularly sharply in 1973, and to Tanzania they virtually ceased. The decline to 1969 was mainly the result of a

TABLE 8.12

Inter-state exports as percentage of exports to all destinations

	1960	1967	1970	1973
Kenya	28	33	31	24
Tanzania	4	5	8	7
Uganda	14	16	12	4

Source: *Annual Trade Reports.*

decline in three products of major importance: raw sugar, cotton-seed oil, and vegetable ghee. These three processed agricultural products, together with cotton fabrics, dominated Uganda's inter-state exports of manufactures. The trade in cotton fabrics was maintained, and a number of more sophisticated manufactures than the staple processed agricultural products came to be exported in increasing amounts. Exports to Kenya from Uganda of a number of manufactures (certain paper products, iron and steel products, tyres and tubes, insulated wire, radio receivers, asbestos cement products, rubber footwear, and cotton yarn) which had accounted for 11 per cent of manufactured exports to Kenya in 1967, had increased their contribution to 21 per cent by 1970, having doubled in value, whereas the proportional importance of the three processed agricultural staples had declined from 36 per cent to 25 per cent. It cannot be assumed that this diversification of Uganda's inter-state exports would have continued in the absence of the political changes which began in January 1971, but at that time the outlook for Uganda's inter-state trade, when account is taken of its changing composition, was not entirely gloomy. New manufactures were being produced and were finding an increasing market within East Africa. The decline in Uganda's exports to the other partner states after 1970 is to be explained by political circumstances and supply constraints rather than by limitations of the market potentially open to Uganda within East Africa.

Although there were setbacks in some years, in general Tanzania enjoyed export success in inter-state trade in manufactures in the years following the Treaty. Her export trade to Uganda is notable mainly for its decline after 1971, from shs. 31m. to shs. 16m. The growth in her manufactured exports to Kenya is noteworthy in two respects: the importance of new products and its dependence on a few products. Total exports of manufactures from Tanzania to Kenya were shs. 57m. greater in 1973 than in 1967. Exports of eight products alone (motor tyres, iron and steel tubes and pipes, aluminium products, fertilizers, clothing, radio receivers, torch batteries, cotton fabrics), which were either non-existent or relatively unimportant in 1967, had increased in value by shs. 47m. in 1973. These characteristics of the development of Tanzania's inter-state trade give grounds both for optimism, in that they show the possibility for the development of trade in new products within the common market, and for concern, in that the growth in trade is dependent on the fortunes of so few products. The susceptibility of the growth of trade to the fortunes of a particular product are well illustrated by cotton fabrics. Exports of cotton fabrics from Tanzania to Kenya were larger in 1973 than in 1967, but they had been even larger in 1971, and had then fallen by two-thirds to the 1973 level. If they had remained at the level reached in 1971 the total increase in exports of manufactures from Tanzania to Kenya between 1967 and 1973 would have been as much as one-third greater than that actually achieved.

The growth of Kenya's inter-state exports of manufactures, although large, was also dependent on a very few products, despite the more developed and diversified structure of Kenya's economy as compared with that of Tanzania. Exports of manufactures to Tanzania were larger in 1973 than in 1967 by shs. 113m.; the increase in three groups of products (processed milk, petroleum products, iron and steel bars and sheets) amounted to more than half of that figure. The increase in Kenya's transfers to Uganda was more widely based than that to Tanzania, but the special circumstances since 1971, with a general shortage of goods in Uganda, must be recognized. Between 1967 and 1970 the increase in transfers from Kenya to Uganda was also narrowly based.

Tanzania levies transfer taxes on about fifty items from Kenya and on nearly thirty from Uganda. Most of the taxes were imposed at the commencement of the transfer-tax system, on 1 December 1967. Uganda levies transfer taxes on some thirty items. Most of the taxes were imposed in 1967; further items were added to the taxed list in 1968 and 1969, and a few more in 1971 and 1972.

Estimates of the value of trade in taxed products before and after the imposition of the transfer taxes are set out in Table 8.13.[14] Transfer taxes were imposed on a relatively small part of the 1967 total inter-state trade in manufactures. By 1972, the taxed proportion of trade in manufactures amounted to 14 per cent for Tanzania's imports from Kenya and 3 per cent for her imports from Uganda, and to 8 per cent for Uganda's imports from Kenya.

Exports of transfer-taxed goods from Kenya to Tanzania not only increased after transfer taxes were imposed, but increased at a faster rate than untaxed exports. In the two other trade flows, however, from Uganda to Tanzania and from Kenya to Uganda, trade in taxed goods declined, particularly in the former, whereas untaxed trade increased (*see* Table 8.14). In each of the three trade flows the changes in taxed

TABLE 8.13

Percentage of inter-state trade in manufactures
subject to transfer taxes imposed in December 1967

	1967	1968	1969
Tanzania from Kenya	16	18	19
Tanzania from Uganda	52	47	9
Tanzania from Kenya and Uganda	23	23	18
Uganda from Kenya	16	8	9

Source: Hazlewood, A., 'Inter-state Trade in Transfer-Taxed Manufactures, 1967–70', East African Statistical Department, *Economic and Statistical Review*, March 1972.

TABLE 8.14

Inter-state trade in goods transfer-taxed in December 1967 and in untaxed goods

	1968	1969
Tanzania from Kenya		
Taxed	136	148
Untaxed	118	123
Tanzania from Uganda		
Taxed	86	14
Untaxed	97	149
Uganda from Kenya		
Taxed	44	54
Untaxed	105	112

NOTE: 1967 = 100

Source: A. Hazlewood, op. cit.

transfers were mainly the result of changes in a very few items. The increase from 1967 to 1968 in taxed exports from Kenya to Tanzania was dominated by increases in soap and detergents, clothing, footwear, and rayon fabrics, these increases being offset to some extent by decreases in cigarettes, and in margarine and cooking fats. In the following year, in contrast, Kenya's exports to Tanzania of margarine and cooking fats increased substantially, and those of clothing, footwear and rayon fabrics decreased. The decline in exports from Uganda to Tanzania of products taxed in 1967 was composed largely of cotton fabrics. In contrast, exports of printed cotton fabrics, which were not taxed until near the end of 1968, increased substantially after the tax was imposed. Most of the decrease in taxed exports from Kenya to Uganda is accounted for by the fall in exports of clothing.

It is clear that no simple relationship exists between the imposition of transfer tax and a change in the value of trade in the taxed products. The influence of the transfer tax on inter-state trade in the first years of the system cannot be deduced from the statistics of the flow of trade. What must be kept in mind in examining the trade changes, however, is that so far as some products are concerned, at least, the imposition of taxes involved a liberalization of trade, because transfer taxes replaced more restrictive quantitative controls.

Since 1970, trade in transfer-taxed products (omitting for statistical consistency the few products taxed in 1970 and later) has developed as shown in Table 8.15.

TABLE 8.15

Transfer-taxed trade, 1970–3

	1971	1972	1973
Tanzania imports	72	64	51
Uganda imports	92	52	128

NOTE: 1970 = 100

Source: East African Statistical Department, *Economic and Statistical Review*, Table D.17.

The Treaty (Article 20.16) provides for the partner states to 'undertake joint consultations to review and reappraise the system five years after the first imposition of a transfer tax'. This reappraisal, which was to be concerned particularly with the effectiveness of the transfer taxes in promoting more balanced industrial development, should have been undertaken during 1973. The partner states agreed, however, that it should be left to each to undertake its own assessment of the system, and no public statement has been made about any conclusions reached. Perhaps it was thought best to let sleeping dogs lie.

Although the common-market provisions of the Treaty are concerned particularly with manufactures, it is of interest to examine the pattern of the remainder of inter-state trade. Table 8.16 shows that the inter-state trade in non-manufactures of both Tanzania and Uganda is more balanced than that in manufactures. But as manufactures constitute a large part of all inter-state trade the more balanced position of the trade in non-manufactures has only a relatively small effect on the overall balance.

The attitude induced by an examination of the post-Treaty history of inter-state trade should be, perhaps, a heavily qualified optimism. Despite transfer taxes and any difficulties created by the introduction of

TABLE 8.16

Inter-state trade in non-manufactures

	shs. m.		
	1967	1970	1973
(a) Value of trade			
Kenya to Tanzania	37	27	33
Kenya to Uganda	48	53	72
Tanzania to Kenya	24	56	54
Tanzania to Uganda	5	7	2
Uganda to Kenya	44	36	25
Uganda to Tanzania	9	7	—
(b) Balance of trade			
Kenya with Tanzania	+13	−29	−21
Kenya with Uganda	+4	+17	+47
Tanzania with Uganda	−4	—	+2

Source: *Annual Trade Reports.*

exchange control and the growth of state trading (*see* Chapter 9), inter-state trade (leaving aside the special circumstances of Uganda) has expanded in value, although by less in real terms as prices have been rising. The trade has become more diversified and somewhat less unbalanced. New products have been introduced into inter-state trade, and some have prospered; processed agricultural products have become less dominant, and more sophisticated manufactures have assumed greater importance. On the other hand there has been no strong and consistently upward trend in inter-state trade. The growth in trade, when it has occurred, has been based on a limited range of products, and the importance of inter-state trade in trade as a whole has declined. Inter-state trade, it may be surmised, rests on a fragile basis and could easily be eroded by developments in domestic production in the partner states for their own markets and in political and economic policies. If inter-state trade is to flourish, it is likely that it will have to derive from a more complex and sophisticated pattern of production specialization between partner states than has hitherto prevailed.

Inter-state trade need not take the form of one state's importing from another only the products of industries which it does not itself possess, otherwise the prospect for inter-state trade would, indeed, be gloomy. It seems improbable that new industries established within East Africa will be set up only in a single state, so that inter-state trade is based on the location of whole industries. On the contrary, it would be surprising if the less industrially advanced states did not develop to a large extent by establishing industries already operating elsewhere in East Africa. There are good reasons why this should be the case. It is likely that the industries found by the industrial leader to be most appropriately and easily established will often be found, for the same reasons, to be those most appropriately and easily established by later industrializers. The 'natural' tendency may be for the late-comers to 'follow the leader'. If this is the case, efficient industrialization within the common market would have to be based on a finer degree of specialization than that of whole industries, and on a pattern of inter-state trade in which a state both exported to and imported from its partners the products of the same industry. Industries in which the different processes and products are closely integrated, and which need to operate on a very large scale, might be an exception to this pattern, and might be located by agreement between the partner states. This matter is considered further in Chapter 9.

NOTES

[1] Published information on the working of the Community is obtainable from newspaper reports (the East African press devotes considerable space to reporting the debates of the EALA and to news of Community affairs at other times); *African Development* (London) also carries reports – and see particularly the Special Survey on the Community, Feb. 1974. Published information is also to be obtained from the annual report of the Community Minister for Common Market and Economic Affairs (see articles by Ouko, R., East African Statistical Dept, *Econ. Statist. R.* March/June 1971, June 1972, June 1973), and from East African Community, *Background to the Budget* (annual since 1973), and Common Market and Economic Affairs Secretariat, *Review of Economic Integration Activities within the East African Community* (annual since 1973). The annual reports of the corporations appear after long delays.

[2] See *Econ. Statist. R.*, Table J.1, and *Background to the Budget, 1973–74*, p. 3.

[3] Hazlewood, A., 'The Territorial Incidence of the East African Common Services', *B. Oxford Univ. Inst. Econ. Statist.*, Aug. 1965.

[4] Due, J. F., and Robson, P., 'Tax Harmonization in the East African Common Market', in Shoup, C. S., (ed.), *Fiscal Harmonization in Common Markets* (New York and London: Columbia University Press, 1966).

[5] See Hazlewood, A., *Rail and Road in East Africa* (Oxford: Blackwell, 1964).

[6] East African Railways Corporation *Annual Report* for 1970.

[7] *Inquiry into the Affairs of East African Airways Corporation by a Select Committee of the East African Legislative Assembly* (Arusha: East African Legislative Assembly, 1973).

[8] *Treaty for East African Co-operation*, Annex XIII, Part A, 4(*f*) relating to the East African Posts and Telecommunications Corporation, and corresponding provisions in the rules relating to the control of the other corporations.

[9] See the discussion of this problem in *Review of Economic Integration Activities within the East African Community, 1973/74*, Chapter IX.

[10] op. cit.

[11] *Background to the Budget, 1973–74*, p. 22.

[12] *Review of Economic Integration Activities within the East African Community, 1973/74*, p. 164.

[13] Parts of this section are based on Hazlewood, A., 'Inter-State Trade in East African Manufactures, 1967–1970', and 'Inter-State Trade in Transfer-Taxed Manufactures, 1967–70', *Econ. Statist. R.*, Sept. 1971 and March 1972. In the East African trade statistics, 'imports' and 'exports' refer to trade between a

partner state and non-members of the Community. Intra-Community or inter-state trade is separately listed as 'goods of East African origin transferred between the partner states'. It is this terminology which gave rise to the term 'transfer tax' for the taxes introduced under the Treaty on certain 'transfers' of the manufactures of one partner state to another. It has seemed more natural in the discussion of this section to use 'exports' and 'imports' for inter-state trade, as well as for external trade, and to distinguish the one from the other in the context of the discussion. There is another sense in which the term 'transfers' is used in the customs administration, to refer to imports into one partner state from outside East Africa, which are subsequently transferred for use in another partner state. There are now no published statistics for such transfers, and the import figures quoted include goods originally imported into another partner state and transferred to the partner state in question.

[14] See Hazlewood, A., op. cit., March 1972, for a discussion of the statistical problems involved in producing consistent series for transfer-taxed trade.

9 *Unsettled Problems*

The previous chapter dealt with developments since the Treaty in some major fields of Community activity. This chapter continues the discussion of the post-Treaty experience of East African integration, but with less emphasis on the description of developments in Community affairs, and more on the analysis of problems which remain unresolved. It is inevitable that problems arise in the operation of so complex a set of political and economic arrangements as those established by the Treaty. East African integration should be seen as a dynamic process, adapting to deal with problems as they arise, not as an unchanging collection of rules and institutions established in 1967. The operation of the Treaty and changes in the national economies have revealed a number of ways in which new initiatives for co-operation are required if the Community is to progress and to achieve more fully the general aims of the Treaty.

(A) INDUSTRIAL CO-ORDINATION AND PLANNING

The Treaty established a régime for what we have called a 'regulated' customs union (Chapter 2). The regulation was to be effected mainly through market forces. Within the protection afforded by the common external tariff, free trade between the partner states was to be limited by transfer taxes so as to protect manufacturing in the less-developed states 'with the aim of promoting industrial balance' (Treaty, Article 20.1). The operation of the market was further to be regulated by the influence of fiscal incentives for industrial development, the partner states having agreed to 'use their best endeavours to agree upon a common scheme' (Treaty, Article 19).

The individual partner states offer a variety of fiscal incentives to investors. They include an investment deduction against tax in addition to the full depreciation allowance, remissions and refunds of duty on imported raw materials, and drawbacks of duty on the imported content of exported manufactures. Dividends paid to non-resident shareholders are tax-free. These measures are largely directed at reducing the costs of an investor, rather than the tax liability on his profits, as in tax-holiday schemes, which have not been adopted in East Africa. The kinds of incentives offered differ little between the partner states, because they are mainly given under the common tax laws. However, the remissions and refunds of import duty are granted at the discretion of the individual partner state, and there is a belief that practice varies, Kenya being more generous than the others. There is also widespread dissatisfaction at the delays involved in obtaining the benefits granted.

The Treaty does not make entirely clear the purposes it was intended a common scheme of fiscal incentives should serve. A common scheme could be designed to be 'neutral', preventing any interference with the operation of the other mechanisms of the common market. It could be designed, for example, to prevent Kenya from offering so much more attractive incentives than Tanzania that the effect of the transfer taxes and the EADB in encouraging industrial development in Tanzania were offset. Or it could be designed to prevent competition between the partner states in the offer of fiscal benefits to investors from which each of them would lose. However, fiscal incentives are dealt with in Chapter V of the Treaty, which is concerned with measures to promote balanced industrial development. It is therefore not unreasonable to assume that the scheme was intended positively to contribute to balanced industrial development rather than to be simply neutral. It could do this by rules which permitted a less-developed partner state to provide more favourable terms to attract investors, without fear that there would be competitive offers by a more-developed partner state.

After some delay a report on fiscal harmonization was commissioned and prepared. It was one of the victims of the slowing-down of Community activity after 1971, and decisions on the proposals in the report and on their implementation have not been made.

The question of fiscal incentives, which include the various exemptions from and drawbacks of import duty, is closely connected with that of the level and structure of the external tariff, which is a major instrument of industrial protection. (Import restrictions and the practices of state trading organizations make it impossible to say that the tariff is *the* major instrument of protection.) It is nowadays widely recognized that the rates of import duty in a customs tariff do not necessarily indicate the rates of protection afforded to domestic production.[1] Particularly if the import content of domestic production is high, and if there is a variety of tariff rates and many exemptions, protection may be much greater than the tariff rates indicate, and may vary widely from industry to industry without logical pattern or intention. The tariff may also result in a serious discrimination against exporters, by increasing their costs and reducing the profitability of export markets in relation to the domestic market. Such considerations lay behind the decision to examine in detail the structure and effects of the East African tariff. It was hoped that such a study would help the design of a more efficient system of protection. No action on an East African basis has been announced, but the Kenya Government declared that it intended to adopt gradually a more even tariff structure.[2] This would reduce the divergence between the tariff rates and the rates of 'effective protection' and reduce the discrimination against exporters. It must be presumed that Kenya did not have unilateral action in mind.

The Treaty does not confine itself entirely to regulatory measures which operate through the market. The East African Development Bank must administer its investments so as to distribute them between the partner states in the proportions laid down in the Treaty. A strong element of market control is retained by the requirement that 'the Bank shall be guided by sound banking principles in its operations and shall finance only economically sound and technically feasible projects' (Charter, Article 13(a)), but if enough investment opportunities exist which satisfy these requirements the Bank can be an instrument of administrative planning to favour the less-developed partner states. Chapter 8 showed that the Bank has successfully operated in this way, so far as the evidence of its first five years can indicate. On the other hand, it was also concluded that the Bank did not seem to have done much to increase the complementarity of the economies of the partner states. In principle, however, the Bank could serve as an important instrument in implementing a plan for the development of industries to serve the whole East African market, if the partner states ever agreed on such a plan.

Another instrument for industrial planning by administrative means rather than through the market existed in the industrial licensing system. Under the industrial licensing legislation, the main purpose of which was to encourage investment in industry serving the regional market, scheduled products could be manufactured only under licence from the East African Industrial Council. In considering applications for a licence the Council had to pay attention, among other matters, to 'the potential production of, and the potential demand for . . . the scheduled articles', and 'the general promotion and development of industries and the avoidance of uneconomic competition' with 'the object of effecting on an East African basis the orderly promotion and development of industries . . .' The cotton textile industry was the first to be scheduled when the legislation came into force in 1948, and only a few industries were added to the list. The licensing system, at the time of the Treaty, applied to cotton and woollen textiles, glass, steel drums, metal doors and windows, and enamel hollow-ware.

The Raisman Commission had been unsympathetic to the use of the licensing system as an instrument of industrial development planning, and it did not fit easily into the market-oriented regulatory scheme of the Treaty. Under the Treaty industrial licensing was to continue, but only until 1973, when the existing licences expired, and no new industries were to be scheduled.

Whatever utility the licensing system might have possessed in the context of an agreed programme for the development of industries to serve the regional market, in practice it failed to achieve its object of orderly industrial development to serve the whole East African market, without wasteful multiplication of production plants. The textile industry illustrates the failure of the system. Free access to the East African market was restricted by transfer taxes and the purchasing policies of state trading organizations, and production capacity multiplied so that excess capacity in some product lines became a serious problem.

Even in the middle of 1973 there were still hopes within the Community Secretariat that the licensing system could be revivified and converted into an important instrument for industrial planning and co-ordination.[3] But such hopes were disappointed, and as no steps were taken by the partner states to prolong the system it expired later that year.

It was concluded in Chapter 7 that the effect of the transfer-tax system on large-scale industries was uncertain. Doubt was thrown on the validity of the implied distinction between, on the one hand, industries which could operate efficiently to serve the market of a single state, and which could be fostered by transfer taxes without serious loss of efficiency and, on the other hand, large-scale industries which required the market of at least two states to operate with tolerable efficiency and in which the multiplication of producing plants would be prevented by the excess capacity and high costs that would result. The fear was expressed that under the Treaty arrangements there could be a multiplication of plants with very severe losses of scale economies.

The experience of the transfer taxes is not easy to interpret. There has been considerable industrial development in Tanzania since the Treaty, and a number of enterprises previously serving the Tanzanian market from Kenya have begun production in Tanzania. It is not certain that this phenomenon has been the consequence of transfer taxes rather than of other causes to any considerable extent (for example, the pre-Treaty quotas and fears that they might be reimposed, import licensing, and exchange control). And it has done little to affect the predominance of Kenya as the manufacturing centre of East Africa. What is quite clear is that duplication of producing plants and the growth of excess capacity have not been avoided. The tyre factories in Kenya and Tanzania and the excess capacity in the textile industry are illustrations. There is, therefore, a case for supplementing, or even replacing, the mechanism of the Treaty if efficient and co-ordinated industrial development is to be fostered.

It is wrong to say, as is sometimes said, that the Treaty made no provision for the planning and co-ordination of industrial development. Certainly, it laid down no specific rules to be followed. In contrast with integration arrangements in some other parts of the world, there is no provision for special régimes for 'integration industries' or for the allocation of such industries between the states. No doubt the then-recent failure of the Kampala Agreement deterred the members of the Philip Commission from recommending such arrangements. In any case, their limited success where they have been tried does not suggest that the Treaty would necessarily have been more useful if it had included such provisions. However, the Treaty did provide in the Economic Consultative and Planning Council a mechanism for consideration of these matters, and through which it would be possible for an agreement on specific action to be negotiated.

It is true that the functions of the ECPC as laid down in the Treaty relate to the planning of the Community services and to assistance with the national planning of the partner states. However, the functions appear to have been interpreted broadly enough to embrace what might be called inter-state planning. It was said in Chapter 8 that the work of the Council has been supported by the establishment of committees of senior officials of the Community and the partner states, including the Committee of Planners, which has concerned itself with the co-ordination and planning of industrial development on an East African basis, that is, with the question of so-called 'multi-national industries'. Studies by the Common Market and Economic Affairs Secretariat of the Community and by consultants have provided material for the discussion of such issues as the criteria that might be used in devising a programme for the development and location of multi-national industries in general and for particular industries. Preliminary studies have been made of a number of large-scale, capital-intensive industries which might be developed to serve an integrated East African market: iron and steel, automobile assembly, and chemicals, including fertilizers and pharmaceuticals. The problems of rationalization in the textile industry have also been studied.

It cannot be expected that these studies should provide detailed and definitive programmes for industrial development, including recommendations for the location of various activities, which would be likely to receive ready acceptance. But it is probable that further progress with the formulation of a programme for multi-national industries cannot be made by further studies without there being political decisions. There are doubtless matters of substance which would make agreement difficult, but the difficulties are compounded by the failure of the Community machinery to operate effectively. It seems highly unlikely that there could be serious consideration of, let alone agreement for action on, these difficult and complicated matters unless the more general problems affecting the operation of the Community were overcome.

One difficulty that has to be faced in any agreement on industrial allocation, and which in discussion of joint planning is too often glossed over, is the likelihood of a conflict between an acceptable allocation of production plants between the partner states and an optimal location of plants from the point of view of production efficiency. The Kampala Agreement paid no attention to locational efficiency. But that was an emergency arrangement, and the longer-term scheme that was foreseen in the agreement did provide for the advice of a committee of industrial experts which would take account of locational efficiency. One possible way round the difficulty that has been suggested, which would be consistent with the pursuit of closer integration and for which there are precedents in East Africa in the corporations of the Community, would be the joint participation by the partner-state governments in the ownership of industrial manufacturing companies. As each partner state would have an interest in the success of such companies, there would be an incentive to agree on their being established in the most efficient location, and to give their products unrestricted access to the whole East African market. Such a scheme would presumably involve the transfer of capital from a less- to a more-developed partner state (how else would the share of ownership by the less-developed be acquired?), which would be an odd contribution to equalization. Moreover, experience of the corporations, which are jointly owned in this way, shows that the partner states are not entirely swayed by considerations of efficiency. And such a system, in which the fruits of industrial development are distributed between the partner states instead of the industries themselves, has been tried before in the form of the Raisman Distributable Pool. The distribution of the fruits of development through payments from the Distributable Pool was rather less direct a distribution than could take place in a scheme for jointly owned manufacturing companies, because it operated indirectly through the effect of development on income-tax and customs revenues. But the two arrangements are not so far removed from each other that one can be optimistic that jointly owned companies are a complete answer to the industrial-location problem.

The conflict between equitable and efficient location could be minimized if decisions on particular plants or industries were taken in association with decisions for a wide range of other industries. Equity could then be satisfied by the allocation of industries the efficiency of which is insensitive to location, and of industries for which locational efficiency and equity are not in conflict. The difficulties of industrial allocation which were discussed in Chapter 2 should, however, be recalled.

(B) STATE TRADING AND INTER-STATE PLANNING[4]

A notable development in the period since the signing of the Treaty has been the growth in importance of state trading organizations in the partner states with a monopoly of the right to import goods both from other partner states and from outside. The importance of 'confinement', as it has come to be known in East Africa, has changed the economic environment in which the mechanisms of the Treaty have to operate, and raises the question of their efficacy in the new environment.

In each partner state the importing of a number of goods is confined to a state trading organization. The motive for confinement, the range of products confined, and the administrative procedures of the organizations differ between the partner states. In particular, the Tanzanian State Trading Corporation is primarily an instrument of nationalization, whereas the Kenya National Trading Corporation is concerned with the Africanization of commerce in a private-enterprise context. Initially, the policy in Uganda of confinement to the National Trading Corporation was similar to that in Kenya, but changes introduced in May 1970 seemed designed to bring Uganda nearer to the Tanzanian model. The situation since the beginning of 1971 has again changed.

The Tanzanian State Trading Corporation was originally established to take over the business of a number of companies that had been nationalized. The importing of a number of products from outside East Africa and from the other partner states was confined to the STC in 1967, and the list of confined products was subsequently greatly extended. In addition to the STC, which has now been split up by product handled and by region, there are certain Tanzanian nationalized manufacturing concerns which have the confinement of imports of the goods which they produce: the Tanzanian Shoe Company is one of these, the National Textile Industries Corporation is another. It became the policy that the imports of all manufactures should be confined to para-statal bodies. Some importing of confined goods has been carried out by private concerns which pay a commission to the STC. But in the main the para-statal trading bodies have acted as principals in the import trade, determining themselves what to buy, not simply responding to orders from distributors. The STC has not itself distributed most of the domestic production of confined goods. Domestic production has been distributed through commercial channels, with a commission being paid to the STC. The Second Five-Year Plan document stated that 'the State Trading Corporation will greatly expand its role in the field of internal distribution'. In February 1970 it was announced that the STC would itself take over the wholesaling of all manufactured goods.

In Kenya the import of a number of commodities is confined to the Kenya National Trading Corporation, which appoints distributors for each confined product, with the aim of increasing African participation in trade. The Corporation does very little trading on its own account, but imports in response to requests from the distributors.

The Uganda National Trading Corporation was set up to foster the Africanization of the distributive trade. Products confined to the Corporation were confined irrespective of source, so that the confinement applied equally to imports from outside East Africa, to transfers from the other partner states, and to Ugandan domestic production. The Corporation appointed distributors to handle the actual distribution of the confined products. In May 1970 the administration of external trade was put on a new basis by the establishment of an Export–Import

Corporation which was given a monopoly of all external trade. The Export–Import Corporation announced that it would work initially through the existing export and import firms.

None of the state trading bodies is specifically and explicitly concerned to foster domestic production by restricting imports or transfers from the other partner states. Nevertheless, it is widely believed that the state trading bodies act in a discriminatory manner, favouring their national producers and restricting inter-state trade. There is no doubt that state trading provides a potentially effective means to give complete protection to domestic producers. There are several ways in which the bodies could operate to produce this effect.

A corporation could decide not to import a product because it wished to support the domestic industry, even though the import was cheaper than the domestic product. Similarly, it could decide not to import although the imported product was of better quality or in some way more suitable. It could pursue a policy of adding high mark-ups to imports, or of charging high commission to importers, so that imports were put at a price disadvantage in the domestic market. Administrative procedures for importers could be made so burdensome and lengthy as to constitute a serious barrier to trade. Such a barrier need not, indeed, be deliberately erected; administrative inefficiency can be a highly effective protective device. These procedures could be used to assist domestic production; they could also be used, if so desired, to favour imports from outside against transfers from another partner state.

Some of these procedures are explicitly discriminatory and could in principle be demonstrated as such. With others discriminatory behaviour would be much more difficult to demonstrate clearly. Who is to say, except the purchaser, whether some 'quality difference' (however defined) does or does not outweigh a certain price differential? Quality very often, like beauty, is in the eye of the beholder. It is possible with some standardized products for technical specifications of quality to be laid down, but this is not possible with most manufactures. The subjective elements in the choice between one product and another may lead to a situation in which one partner state feels its products are being discriminated against by the state trading organization of another, whereas that organization is acting in good faith in buying from another source a product which it believes better suits its requirements. Situations of this kind could be the basis of strained relations between the partner states.

It is clearly possible for a body such as the Tanzanian State Trading Corporation, acting as principal in the import trade, to favour domestic producers by importing only enough to meet a domestic supply deficiency (to the extent that it was capable of identifying a deficiency), or when the price difference between the imported and domestically produced product was thought to be excessive. In products the imports of which are confined to the domestic producer it might well seem to those concerned to be the natural procedure to import only when demand exceeded what they could produce themselves.

A body, such as the KNTC, which normally responds to the orders of distributors, is not in so obviously a strong position to discriminate against imports. Nevertheless, it is widely believed that the activities of the KNTC do favour Kenya producers as against those of the other partner states, and some cases have been taken to the Common Market Council. One way they could have this effect is by restricting the channels of distribution for imported goods. To the extent that domestic goods are not restricted to KNTC-appointed distributors their distribution network is likely to be wider than that available to imports.

Under the Treaty all quantitative restrictions (with the exceptions noted in Chapter 7) were to be removed, and it may have been expected that import licensing would cease to apply to inter-state trade. This did not prove to be the case; specific licensing continued, though it was argued that it was not being used restrictively. The purpose of the licensing system as applied to goods from the other partner states, Tanzania argued, was simply to guarantee that they were confined to para-statal bodies and could not be brought into Tanzania by any other importer. Uganda also continued licensing, maintaining that it was necessary to provide statistical information. Eventually it was agreed that licensing itself was not incompatible with the Treaty, but that inter-state transfers should be subject only to 'open general licences' which did not impose any restrictions.

There were many complaints in the period following the commencement of the Treaty that inter-state transfers were still being subjected to quantitative restrictions, and that licences were not being freely given for unlimited quantities. It does not seem improbable that for a time officials continued to enforce the old restrictions. This may have been because of a lack of experience and understanding, or because of mistaken zeal on the part of junior officials. It is said by some (though denied by others) that the Tanzanian STC had a policy of purchasing a domestic product if its price was not more than 20 per cent greater than the import price, and that at one time this rule was mistakenly applied to transfers from the other partner states. It is also not improbable that during the 'teething troubles' of the new arrangements, including the transfer of distribution into inexperienced hands, the distribution of goods in general, and not only of goods transferred in inter-state trade, was hampered. But complaints continued that licensing of inter-state transfers was being used restrictively. It was alleged, for instance, that applications by Uganda distributors for licences to import goods from Kenya had been returned to them marked 'buy Ugandan', or had been granted only for a smaller quantity than had been applied for.

The state trading organizations of the partner states could reduce the function of inter-state trade in each and every product to that of filling deficiencies in domestic supply during the time needed to reach self-sufficiency. If state trading were to operate in this way, inter-state trade would decline as the industrial structure and domestic production expanded in each partner state and as self-sufficiency was approached. The benefits of scale and specialization within the common market would be lost and the main basis of the Community would be eroded. Inter-state trade might for a time revive as new products, not previously produced in East Africa, came to be established in one of the partner states, and until production was established in the others, but it is difficult to see much of a future for a common market in which this was the sole basis for trade. It is obviously vital, if the common market is to operate in the manner envisaged in the Treaty, that Article 16, which states that one-channel marketing and discriminatory purchasing 'are incompatible with this Treaty to the extent that they frustrate the benefits expected from the removal or absence of duties and quantitative restrictions on trade between the Partner States', should be effective.

A code of behaviour for state trading organizations has been adopted by the Community which is designed to achieve non-discrimination, and to make the market work.[5] If followed, the code would allow state trading bodies, which since the time of the discussions leading to the Treaty have acquired a dominating position that was not perhaps envisaged when Article 16 was drawn up, to operate without frustrating the benefits of free inter-state trade.

It must be recognized, however, that the operation of such rules is not easy. The prevention of overt discriminatory practices presents no difficulty in principle. Though if the barrier to trade lies in the reluctance of a state trading body to accept orders from private distributors for goods from another partner state, it may be that distributors will be disinclined to make complaints against so powerful an organization. And it has already been remarked that the subjective element in the 'quality' of a product makes discrimination in purchasing extremely difficult to prove, and may cause a particular purchase to appear discriminatory from one viewpoint but not from another. This is the kind of issue that might be resolved by reference to the Common Market Tribunal. It may be possible to cause regular purchases to be discontinued in deference to a decision by the Tribunal, but for some purchases an adverse decision of the Tribunal will be very much a matter of shutting the stable door after the horse has bolted.

Perhaps not the least difficulty in the operation of the rules would be the political problem faced by a state trading organization in adhering to them. It has already been suggested that, in those cases where the import of a product is confined to the domestic producer, the producer would find it perfectly natural to import only to meet deficiencies in domestic supply. It would be a very sophisticated manager of such a concern (or a very tightly controlled one) who would run his productive capacity at below the maximum and restrict the growth of the industry so as to buy from another partner state. It is easier to envisage a state trading organization, which is not itself a producer, buying the products of another partner state rather than the more expensive, or poorer quality, or less suitable products of a domestic producer. An organization concerned with its own financial success, and operating on a directive to concern itself with that, rather than with other 'national' objectives, could be envisaged as functioning in this 'profit maximizing' manner. There does, therefore, seem to be a significant difference in the likely effect on inter-state trade of confinement to a domestic producer and confinement to a non-producing state trading organization. Nevertheless, it would be wrong to ignore the difficulties that a state trading organization would face in concerning itself simply with its success as a trader. Such behaviour would imply that it would be prepared to create excess capacity and unemployment and restrict expansion in a domestic industry by choosing to buy from another partner state. The political obstacles to such behaviour would be severe.

It is an arguable proposition that the Treaty, because of the development of state trading, is already out of date, and indeed began to become out of date from when it came into force. The Treaty established a régime for a common market of market economies. Under the Treaty trade takes place according to market criteria, according, that is, to market prices, as influenced by the transfer taxes. Development takes place according to market criteria, as influenced by a common system of fiscal incentives and by the activities of the East African Development Bank. The operation of one-channel marketing and other arrangements in a way inconsistent with the achievement of the benefits expected from free trade within the common market is banned, and the code of behaviour for state trading organizations is designed to make them behave as if they were operating in a competitive market according to market criteria. When trade and commerce, and particularly the import trade, have been removed to an important extent from the sphere of the market, it is arguable that provisions for a 'common market of market economies' are no longer entirely relevant, nor can they be made relevant by imposing rules to simulate the market. The question arises, then, for this reason as well as for those discussed in the previous section of this chapter, as to whether the future of the common market lies not in the régime of the market but in the régime of planning.

The discussion in the previous section of this chapter was concerned with planning as a way of preventing the uneconomic multiplication of production plants and of securing an acceptable location of large-scale industries. However, it may not be realistic to assume that any one of the partner states will be prepared indefinitely (or for so long a period as there would be no loss of economies in duplication of productive facilities) to deny itself any industry that it could attract or establish. Perhaps there are some industries the characteristics of which would enable a single plant, but not more than a single plant, to operate within the East African market, and these might be the subject of an allocation agreement between the partner states. But an agreement which dealt with these industries alone would go only part of the way to avoiding the costs of small-scale production. An agreement would need to be more far-reaching and to lead to a more sophisticated pattern of specialization between the partner states.

What is required as the basis for a flourishing and beneficial common market in the future is a pattern of *intra*-industry specialization, as a result of which even though each partner state had 'every' industry there was mutually beneficial trade between the partner states on the basis of specialization on particular grades, qualities, styles, components, etc. Specialization *between* industries appears the natural or only basis of specialization only so long as an 'industry' is thought of as the producer of a single, homogeneous product. Typically, however, industries are multi-product producers, so that specialization *within* industries offers greater possibilities than that between industries, and there is every reason to expect that beneficial exchange can take place between countries with what appear to be similar industrial structures. If it were not so, it would follow that trade between countries would decline as they became more industrially developed; in fact, the opposite is found to be the case. Many more industries will have an optimum size which is large in relation to the size of the market in East Africa than in the developed countries, so that intra-industry specialization is particularly desirable.

At a low level of development it may be costly to operate more than one plant in an industry, even though there is a measure of specialization between them. The magnitude of the costs and benefits of multiplication of plants, and specialization, as well as the possibility of and the basis for specialization, obviously vary from industry to industry. But if the alternative to specialization, as in reality it is often likely to be, is not the concentration of production in a single plant, but the operation of more than one plant *without* specialization, specialization will be the more efficient arrangement. And it seems fairly clear that in many industries there will be substantial economies to be obtained if, as the market for the industry expands and additional plants are established, they specialize on the basis of the East African market, rather than each producing a wider range of products for the national market alone. Such a pattern of specialization should be possible without its being based on the artificial stimulation of variety, brand preference, etc., which East Africa cannot afford. The establishment of such a pattern of specialization might be reflected in a pattern of inter-state trade in which, as was foreseen in Chapter 8, a partner state is both an importer and an exporter of the 'same' product.

It is not inconceivable that specialization of the kind required could develop through the pressures of the market by way of market-sharing agreements between private producers. The growth of such arrangements would be the more likely the more frequently the productive capacity in the different partner states was under the ultimate control of the same company. It must be said, however, that the transfer-tax system may discourage such arrangements, unless the taxable products are narrowly defined, and they certainly could not be relied upon to develop fully through the play of market forces, particularly with market forces superseded to so large an extent by the activities of state-trading organizations. In the situation created by the importance of state trading there can be little doubt that intra-industry specialization between the partner states can develop only within the context of an agreement between the partner states on production specialization which in addition regulates the purchasing policy of the state trading organizations. An agreement under which specialization is fostered may be the only alternative to the growth of national autarky and the withering away of the common market. Under a régime of planning, state trading could become a device for implementing the plan and for associating an agreed specialization of production with an expansion of intra-Community trade. But the planning could not take the form of a once-for-all allocation of industries; it would have to be the continuous co-ordination of the dynamic process of industrial development.

(C) TRANSPORT CO-ORDINATION AND PLANNING

Cheap and efficient transport between the member countries is of enormous importance in a common market if it is to be more than a formality. The abolition of artificial restraints on trade between the members is of little relevance if the natural restraints are high. East Africa is fortunate in possessing a transport 'infra-structure' linking the three countries that is relatively well developed and provides closer links between the partner states than is usual between contiguous countries in Africa. However, this does not mean that further investment in transport is unnecessary, or that there are no possibilities for improvement in the structure and utilization of transport facilities.

A difficulty facing the co-ordination and planning of surface transport on an East African basis is created by the fact that railways are a Community responsibility whereas the provision of roads and the regulation of road transport are a matter for the individual partner states. The development of roads and road transport has been primarily directed towards the provision of transport within each partner state rather than between them. Perhaps the outstanding illustration is the fact that a tarred road, running parallel with the railway, was completed between Mombasa and Nairobi several years before such a road existed between Nairobi and Arusha, where there was no convenient rail link.

Given the difference in the control over railways and roads, one field of activity in which there is clearly scope for co-ordination is investment in transport.[6] Because investment is necessarily a Community matter for railways, the Community cannot neglect the matter of investment in roads. It is not a straightforward matter, because the Community controls investment in railway vehicles as well as in railway track and installations; the partner-state governments undertake investment in roads, but a large part of the investment in vehicles is in private hands. The planning of transport investment through the Community machinery will not, therefore, in the case of railways and roads, be concerned with activities of completely comparable scope. Even so, it is highly desirable that decisions on investment in roads should not be taken in one partner state entirely independently and in ignorance of decisions on road investment in another partner state and on investment in railways by the Community. If correct decisions are to be made it is essential that the benefits of any particular investment should be judged in the light of the alternative investment possibilities. For example, investment in railway wagons, lorries, and storage facilities would almost certainly be more beneficial than investment in new railway routes, as favoured by Tanzania. But it is difficult to ensure that governments do give proper consideration to investment alternatives, and it is even more difficult when railway investment is in the hands of an authority operating over the whole of East Africa and investment in roads is the responsibility of the individual governments. In principle, it is less difficult since the inauguration of the Community. The Treaty provides in the Communications Council 'a forum for consultation generally on communications matters' (Article 55), and the Council and its secretariat have not confined themselves to matters narrowly concerning the Corporations of the Community. Nevertheless, the co-ordination and planning carried out through the Community institutions falls a long way short of providing an East African plan for the development of surface transport. The report of the ambitious East African Transport Study commissioned by the three governments and the World Bank in 1967 seems to have been shelved.

Co-ordination of the regulation and control of road transport by the different partner states is important for two reasons. One is the desirability of preventing the regulation of road transport from inhibiting inter-state trade. The other is the desirability of preventing regulation from interfering with an economic distribution of traffic between road and rail and thereby interfering with the efficient utilization of transport facilities. Potential barriers to free movement across state boundaries have grown up in the form of vehicle-licensing regulations and charges, and tolls levied at border crossings. A Community study of the legislative provisions for regulating road transport found that they are, indeed, likely to jeopardize the free exchange of goods across state borders. Further studies are under way, and efforts to secure closer harmonization of policies towards road transport continue. The Community recognizes, however, that 'co-ordinated planning and decision-taking in the sphere of road transportation has not gone very far'.[7]

A major aim of transport policy is to achieve, so far as possible, an allocation of traffic between road and rail under which traffic is carried by the least-cost method. It might be possible to achieve such an economic distribution of traffic by administrative regulation and control. It can hardly be thought that, in general, the restrictions on road transport that operated in East Africa were sufficiently discriminating to achieve such a result. More probably they increased the cost of transport and inhibited development. In any case, the restrictions have been greatly relaxed and the railway revenue has suffered in consequence. In the absence of administrative regulation, and assuming carrying capacity is available in both, the allocation of traffic between road and rail must be largely dependent on the prices charged by the two forms of transport. If an economic allocation is to be achieved these prices must reflect costs. Road-haulage charges will not reflect costs if taxation does not impose on road hauliers the cost of the provision and maintenance of the roads, and for this to be done on an East African basis the road-taxation and licensing policies of the partner states must be similar. The level of taxation need not be the same throughout East Africa, because road costs may differ from place to place, but the policy of imposing the costs of the road on road users must be applied by each of the governments. Until more progress has been made in the co-ordination of road-transport policy an economic distribution of traffic and utilization of transport facilities will be difficult to achieve.

The co-ordination of road-transport policy and the adoption of an appropriate structure of taxation of road users will not achieve an economic distribution of traffic between road and rail unless the railway tariff also reflects the costs of providing rail transport. In the past the charges in the railway tariff were not based on the cost of carrying particular traffics. Some traffics were carried at less, and others at more than they cost. This cross-subsidization was a matter of contention between the countries, because of the different degree to which it was believed it affected them. Broadly, the railway tariff charged low rates for exports and high rates for imports, and it had a 'taper' so that the cost per mile for a long haul was below that for a short haul. There are few hard facts on which to base any conclusion about the tariff's inter-territorial impact, but it is certain that it was accidental rather than deliberate. Even the cross-subsidization between products was accidental, for the lower rates for exports than for imports did not necessarily mean that the former were subsidized, because they might have been cheaper to carry. One study came to the conclusion that this was, in fact, the case.[8] There have been some moves towards changes in the structure of the railway tariff towards charges which are more closely related to cost, but the full implications of using tariffs and taxes to achieve an economic allocation of traffic between road and rail have not been faced.

It is perfectly reasonable for governments to wish to use transport as an instrument of economic policy, and to foster development or to favour particular traffics or regions by subsidies. If such subsidization is to be given within the railway finances, by attempting to pay for the losses on some traffics by higher charges on others, the highly charged traffics may be attracted away to road transport, even though the economic cost by road is higher than by rail. A way needs to be found, therefore, in which transport pricing can be used as an instrument of economic policy without distorting the efficient allocation of traffic between road and rail.

It would be possible for the subsidies to be provided from the budget of a partner state, and this is what the 'branch-line formula' in the Treaty envisages for unremunerative new services which the railway is asked to provide. In Chapter 8 it was said that the formula had not been effective in protecting the railways from pressure for unremunerative expansion, and in any case it seems improbable that the budgetary situation in the partner states would allow for subsidization of transport to any great extent.

The railway is a carrier of petroleum products in bulk over long distances at lower cost than road transport. This traffic could be charged at a high rate, so as to provide for cross-subsidization of other traffics, and be prohibited to road transport, without interfering with the economic distribution of traffic between road and rail. However, developments have been in the opposite direction: road haulage of petroleum products has been allowed to grow and the railway has had to lower its charges for, and reduce the profitability of this traffic in order to compete. It may be wondered whether a complete reversal of this trend would be politically possible. Such a policy would also be ruled out by the decision taken in 1974 to construct an oil pipeline inland from Mombasa. Unless this were to be restricted to conveying traffic in excess of the carrying capacity of the railways for bulk oil, the prospect for the railways' finances seem very serious indeed. As it happened, partly because of the general disorganization in the Corporation, and partly because of an earlier error in forecasting demand and a failure to expand tank-wagon capacity sufficiently, in 1974 and some earlier years the railways were unable to carry all the petroleum traffic that they could have attracted. Nevertheless, this does not alter the fact that, in normal circumstances, the loss of bulk oil traffic would be the loss of what in the past had been the railways' most remunerative traffic.

A third way of financing transport subsidies would be to raise taxes from both road and rail (and from the pipeline, if it is constructed), so as not to influence the distribution of traffic between them, and to subsidize the traffics it is desired to subsidize, whether they are carried by road or by rail.

All these issues of transport policy require closer co-ordination and planning by the partner states than has yet been achieved if there is to be efficient utilization and development of transport in East Africa.

(D) AGRICULTURE AND THE COMMON MARKET[9]

The major reason for the exclusion of trade in agricultural products from the common-market provisions of the Treaty was the incompatibility of free inter-state trade with the national marketing arrangements and control of internal trade for some products of major importance. Nevertheless, the Treaty commits the partner states to the establishment of a common market in agricultural products in the long run. The importance of achieving this aim depends on what benefits might accrue from an East African common market in agricultural produce.

One of the main arguments for a common market in manufactures – the existence of economies of scale in production – is not of much relevance to East African agriculture. The benefits of a larger market area are more likely to be found in the scope for realizing natural advantages in the location of production. But it is not clear how important are the gains to be achieved through specialization between the countries according to natural advantage. The variability of natural conditions affecting agriculture is perhaps as great within as between the countries. Kenya is certainly relatively well endowed for the production of temperate agricultural products, but her superiority in dairy products, meat, and wheat may be as much the result of her 'infra-structure' in these industries (including technical knowledge and the existence of measures for disease control as well as processing, marketing, and transport facilities) as of the 'natural' environment. Even where there appear to be important locational advantages in one of the countries for a particular product, this is not a conclusive indication of potential gains from specialization and free trade. Although another country may not be naturally well suited to the product, its opportunity-cost of production may nevertheless be low, for the alternative may be an even less productive use of land and labour.

If specialization were to take place according to natural (and acquired) advantage one country would normally be in surplus and another in deficit in a particular crop. Surpluses and deficits which were seasonal and erratic could also be superimposed on the normal pattern. Differences in the seasonal pattern of production in a particular crop could provide a basis for beneficial inter-state trade. Even though two of the countries were self-sufficient in the crop on average over the year, they might each benefit from importing at one time of the year and exporting at another. It has been said that the agricultural pattern in East Africa is such that if trade were uncontrolled, 'food crops would tend to move northwards in the April–May period, and southwards in the July–September period, thus reducing the costs of storage, wastage, etc. in each area'.[10]

The actual pattern of production within East Africa is affected by chance climatic and other natural conditions. A harvest failure (or glut) in a particular country could lead to its being in deficit (surplus) when it is normally in surplus (deficit). Beneficial trade between the countries could arise from such erratic supply-fluctuations, allowing their impact to be reduced.

Differences in natural advantage do not necessarily provide a basis for beneficial specialization and trade. The benefits from seasonal exchanges depend on the extent of the seasonal differences and on the relative cost of transport and storage, and this is liable to change through technical innovation. The possibility of diminishing the impact of erratic fluctuations through inter-state trade depends on the extent to which the natural fluctuations are felt in one country alone or over East Africa as a whole. If all countries were to suffer drought at the same time there would not be much to be gained from trade. It might be expected that the larger the area the less likely it would be for all parts to experience the same abnormal weather conditions at the same time, and it is said that Uganda is less liable to erratic conditions than Kenya and Tanzania. There are undoubtedly potential benefits in inter-state trade in agricultural products. It is not improbable, however, that greater gains would derive from changes affecting the market within the partner states – freer internal trade and changes in pricing policies, for example – which might in any case be a precondition of the extension of the common market to agriculture. It has been said that

> Kenya's most serious marketing problems are . . . that the system stifles initiative at the vital lower levels, that it still discriminates severely between different producer groups, that it protects producers at the expense of consumers in some important cases, and that it fails particularly in its price policies to make the most of the agricultural potential Kenya has.[11]

The difficulty of achieving a freer internal market no doubt varies between crops and between countries. It may be presumed that the social philosophy of Tanzania would favour control. In Kenya, the difficulty might depend, for some crops, on the readiness with which the government is prepared to remove protection from the producers or to replace quantitative restrictions with subsidies. For maize a free market would require the abandonment of long-established marketing controls, the nominal restrictiveness of which is indicated by the fact that it is illegal without a permit to move more than ten bags of maize within a district, or two bags outside a district. However, the control system has been breaking down, and for this reason, as well as because of its inherent disadvantages, a Select Committee of the National Assembly recommended in the middle of 1973 that the system should be abandoned and a free market in maize established within Kenya.[12] The Committee took the view that it would be an advantage if the maize market could be organized on an East African basis, but did not consider that this was feasible at the time. However, if their recommendation is adopted it would at least remove one obstacle in the way of the establishment of an East African market in maize.

Even when it is formally honoured, the Treaty commitment to an extension of the common market to agriculture may not, in fact, lead to genuine free trade in agricultural products. Article 14 commits the countries to a common market in agricultural produce but also to 'co-operation and consultation in the field of agricultural policy', and it refers to 'trade arrangements between the national agencies and marketing boards'. It is not impossible that co-operation on agricultural policy and arrangements between the national marketing boards could lead to a situation in which prices are set so that there is no incentive for trade to take place between the countries, or in which monopoly marketing agencies do not trade. The importance of organized marketing and the emphasis on national self-sufficiency suggests that Article 14 could be interpreted in this way. Such arrangements would ease the removal of quantitative restrictions, but they might also remove the benefits of an extension of the Common Market to 'agriculture and trade in agricultural products'.

Beneficial co-operation between the partner states is possible over policies towards export crops and international agreements. Knowledge of the agricultural situation can be increased by an improvement in statistics and by studies carried out by the Community. Schemes for crop storage on an East African basis and for a system of 'first call' on the other partner states in meeting seasonal and irregular deficiencies can be devised. Of course, co-operation could be carried further and a planned approach to self-sufficiency on an East African basis substituted for the policies of national self-sufficiency now being pursued. But whether the market approach of the Treaty or a planning approach is the more practicable, the development of co-operation in agricultural production and trade is a substantial piece of unfinished business for the partner states.

(E) MONETARY CO-OPERATION

The monetary situation in East Africa at the time the Treaty was signed was very different from that of three years later. In 1967 the three central banks had only just opened their doors for business. The three currencies were still virtually identical. Transfers between the partner states could be made with complete freedom, the currency of each state could be used without difficulty for transactions in the other states, and notes (not coins) could be freely exchanged. There had been a hint of things to come early in 1967. In February, following the nationalization of the banks in Tanzania, exchange control was imposed by Tanzania against Kenya and Uganda as part of measures adopted to restrict capital flight, and the free circulation and redemption of Tanzanian notes in the other states was suspended. But it was only a temporary break in the *de facto* monetary union, and the restrictions were lifted in June.

The consultative machinery on monetary matters established under the Treaty survived a test early in its life when, in November 1967, following the sterling devaluation, it was agreed that the three currencies should maintain their par value and should not follow sterling. The link with sterling was severed, but the three currencies maintained their rate of exchange with each other.

In 1970, the monetary union was disrupted more severely than in 1967. There had been a heavy outflow of capital from Uganda, particularly after a Presidential announcement on nationalization policy, and early in May Uganda imposed exchange control against Kenya and Tanzania and banned the export and import of Uganda currency, which ceased to be redeemable elsewhere in East Africa. No reciprocal steps were taken at that time by the other partner states. The Central Bank of Kenya 'hoped that these measures will soon be removed in accordance with the spirit of the Treaty for East African Co-operation',[13] but it was not to be. On the contrary, less than a year later, in March 1971, Tanzania followed Uganda's example and imposed similar restrictions. A few days afterwards, to prevent speculation, Kenya made it illegal to export or import Kenya currency, including transfers to and from Tanzania and Uganda. None of these restrictions on the freedom of monetary transactions within East Africa was later removed.

The restrictions were specifically directed at the outflow of capital. The control of capital movements by a partner state is permissible under the Treaty, so long as, in a somewhat ambiguous phrase, control 'is necessary for furthering its economic development and an increase in trade consistent with the aims of the Community', and so long as control does not 'prejudice the ability of the Community, the Bank or the Corporations' to perform their functions (Article 25). A refusal to exchange the currency notes of another partner state would seem to be a violation of the Treaty (Article 24), but the issue hardly arises if the export of its notes is banned by the government of the other partner state.

After the controls imposed in 1970, the Bank of Uganda confirmed that there were no restrictions on payments to Tanzania and Kenya for financing imports, provided the appropriate procedures were followed. The Kenyan Central Bank, after the controls imposed in March 1971, declared that there were no restrictions on payments or transfers to Uganda and Tanzania so long as they were transacted through the banking system. Tanzania's Minister of Finance, after the imposition of exchange control against Kenya and Uganda, said that only capital transfers to the other partner states that were in the interest of Tanzania's development would be allowed, that all payments were to be scrutinized to ensure that there was no capital hidden in them, but that bona fide current payments for goods and services were not restricted. He also expressed the hope that the administration of exchange control would be such as to minimize delays. It seems unlikely, in practice, that the imposition of exchange control does not delay and diminish legitimate transactions between the partner states. Reference has already been made to the effect of exchange control on the ease with which the funds of the Community corporations can be moved from one part of East Africa to another.

It must not be thought that the consultative machinery established under the Treaty ceased to operate after the exchange controls were introduced. It worked to maintain at least the appearance of monetary harmonization, despite the divergent policies of the partner states. For instance, in August 1971, following the devaluation of the United States dollar, the Tanzanian shilling was pegged to the dollar, whereas, for a time, Kenya and Uganda retained their parity with sterling. For a few days transactions between the partner states were suspended until an agreement emerged under which all three currencies were pegged to the dollar. Since then there have been agreed decisions to alter the exchange rate of all three currencies together, but the parity between them has been maintained. It would be true to say, therefore, that the arrangements for consultation and co-operation envisaged in the Treaty have been effective. The regular meetings of the central-bank Governors have taken place, and they have met additionally when circumstances required it, and have reached agreement. In 1968 the Governor of the Central Bank of Kenya could say with truth that the role of the central banks in East African co-operation was 'to ensure that monetary policies of the three countries move in step, thereby facilitating smooth payments arrangements'.[14] It was not long before it became clear, however, that central-bank co-operation was not enough to prevent disruption in the payments mechanism. And to the extent that co-operation is concerned to maintain the fixed relationship between the three currencies, it could be argued that such co-operation helps to restrict the free flow of transactions within East Africa.

The advantages of fixed exchange-rates between the currencies of the partner states are obvious; the disadvantages do not emerge without more analysis. With fixed exchange-rates transactions are facilitated by the elimination of the 'exchange risk'. It is possible, so far as the relationship between the three currencies is concerned, to treat East Africa as a unified market in a way that would not be possible if there were a risk of the rates of exchange altering. The fact that in East Africa there is a one-to-one relationship between the three shillings is perhaps a minor convenience, but as an additional argument for fixed exchange-rates between the currencies it is trivial. The operations of the corporations and of other institutions operating throughout East Africa are facilitated by the existence of fixed exchange-rates, but it would be a mistake to think that it would be impossible for them to adjust to a situation in which the rates of exchange between the currencies varied.

The argument in favour of fixed rates, the elimination of the exchange risk, would be stronger if there were a common currency in East Africa, issued by a single institution and supported by common foreign-exchange reserves. In these circumstances the exchange risk attaching to intra-East African transactions would, in truth, have been eliminated. But they are not the circumstances. There are three currencies, three institutions, and three separate reserves, so that the possibility of a variation in the exchange-rate cannot be ruled out. The currencies are not identical and are not thought to be identical by the public. One currency can, therefore, come to be preferred to the others, and black-market rates very different from the official parities can emerge.

In East Africa, although the adoption of a sales tax by Kenya in 1973 diminished one divergence, the policies of the partner states in many relevant spheres of activity have become increasingly divergent since 1967. This is particularly so in policies concerning private ownership and investment, and has led to the capital flights from Uganda and Tanzania towards Kenya and the exchange-control measures of 1970 and 1971. Central bankers cannot eliminate the effects of such policy divergences by consulting and co-operating, nor can they eliminate the effects of differences in credit policies, in the growth of the money supply, and in relative cost-levels. They can keep the exchange-rates between the currencies fixed, but perhaps only at the cost of increasingly severe restrictions on transactions between the partner states.

In a single currency area the 'balances of payments' between different parts of the area are adjusted by changes in income and through movements of labour and capital, assisted by any regional assistance and development policies that may exist. There can be no help from changes in the rates of exchange between the areas, because there is a single currency. It is the same in a common market in which the rates of exchange between the currencies are fixed, with the complication that the possibility, despite all declarations to the contrary, that the rates of exchange could be altered will lead at times to speculative capital movements in a disequalizing rather than an equalizing direction. The 'regional policies' of the Treaty – the EADB and the transfer taxes – are thought by many observers in any case to be not particularly effective. It could therefore be argued that the burden put on them should be lightened by allowing adjustments in the rates of exchange of the currencies. One of the important issues facing the Community, therefore, is whether the advantages of fixed rates of exchange between the currencies any longer outweigh the disadvantages.[15]

There is another monetary issue facing the Community which arises from the fact that balances in inter-state trade represent foreign-exchange transfers between the partner states. Deficits below shs. 10m. are settled in local currency, but in excess of that sum in foreign exchange. In times of foreign-exchange difficulties there is as much incentive to restrict imports from the other partner states as from the rest of the world. It is difficult to believe that the commitments of the Treaty are strong enough, when balance-of-payments problems are severe, to make inter-state trade immune from measures to restrict imports. The issue arises, then, as to whether some new device is desirable to foster inter-state trade in an era of foreign-exchange problems. The Treaty has the rudiments of such a device. It is provided that a partner state in balance-of-payments difficulties can obtain credits from a partner state with which it has a payments deficit. The credits are temporary and relatively small. It was remarked in Chapter 7 that the limited nature of this provision would not prevent Kenya from continuing to earn foreign exchange in inter-state trade to set against her deficit in external trade. Given the adverse effects on inter-state trade of the foreign-exchange difficulties of the partner states, it should be considered whether there would not be an advantage, even for Kenya, in some limitation on the convertibility into foreign exchange of the net balances in inter-state transactions.

In 1965 Kenya's surplus in inter-state trade amounted to nearly half of her deficit on external trade. Data on transactions other than commodity trade are not available, but it is clear that the convertibility of her inter-state balance was an enormously important matter for Kenya. In 1973 her inter-state trade surplus still exceeded a third of her external trade deficit. There seems no reason, given these figures, why Kenya should be more willing in the 1970s than she was in the 1960s to see any effective limitation imposed on the convertibility into foreign exchange of her surplus in inter-state trade. On the other hand, she might be persuaded to accept a limitation of convertibility if the alternative were likely to be a serious decline in her inter-state exports. The acceptability of a limitation on full convertibility of inter-state balances would be improved if a way could be found to introduce additional foreign exchange obtained from economic aid sources into an East African payments scheme. What is required is a scheme which restricts or removes the incentive to save foreign exchange by restricting inter-state imports, and which at the same time does not make it impossible for a surplus country in inter-state trade to use at least part of its surplus to set against its external deficit. Such a scheme, though difficult to devise, could become an important new ingredient in the East African arrangements, and its elaboration and negotiation would be a major achievement for the Community.

(F) POLITICAL COMMITMENT

In the light of the problems facing the Community in its existing range of responsibilities, and when nationalistic forces appear to be in the ascendant, it may seem strange that the idea of an East African federation is again being canvassed. At a meeting of the Legislative Assembly at the end of 1973 it was decided to set up a committee to study proposals for an East African federation, to assess public support for federation, and to recommend procedures for discussion and implementation. In fact, talk about federation had never died out. For example, in 1972 a meeting of Community trade unions declared that federation was overdue and called on the Authority 'to do everything possible to bring about a political federation', and the Secretary-General of the Community, while emphasizing the difficulties, remarked that there was majority support for federation among the people of East Africa.

It seems probable that proposals for federation will make no significant progress, and that they will not be taken too seriously by the governments of the partner states. It seems unlikely that the surrender of national sovereignty required in a federation would be acceptable if there were a reluctance to accept the far more limited surrender of sovereignty required by the present arrangements. It may be that federation is seen by its advocates not as a rational and practicable solution to present problems, but rather as a *deus ex machina* which in some unexplained way will solve all difficulties. Nevertheless, the advocacy of federation is an indication of the underlying support for continuing and strengthened East African unity, and the advocates of federation do show an appreciation of the fact that continued and deepened co-operation is dependent on political commitment.

In the 1960s the newly independent East African states inherited integration arrangements that had a long history and a momentum for continuation. But it was not simply inertia that allowed the arrangements to continue. There was a widespread and genuine belief in the desirability of East African unity, most strikingly indicated by the abortive movement towards federation at that time. This feeling for unity is an important reason for the resilience shown by the Community to the strains and stresses to which it is subjected. The importance of their experience of co-operation and their common educational and cultural backgrounds for the feeling for unity among those – politicians and officials – who work the Community institutions should not be underestimated. On the other hand, the inheritance of the integration arrangements from the colonial period could have stimulated an impatience with the constraints of co-operation once the constraints of colonialism had been removed. For it must again be emphasized that co-operation imposes considerable constraints on the freedom of the governments of the individual partner states, and in one way or another the troubles of the Community spring from a reluctance of the governments to accept these constraints.

To criticize the partner states for looking to their own interest is misplaced. That is the job of their governments, and if any one of them saw no national advantage from the Community it would be right to withdraw. Short of withdrawal, it is to be expected that a government should endeavour to manipulate the arrangements to serve its national interest. The political skill demanded by co-operation is the reconciliation of the interests of the individual partner states and those of the Community as a whole, so that each partner state is benefited, and believes itself to be benefited, by co-operating with the others. This is no easy task, and it is not to be expected that it can be achieved without strains and stresses and hard bargaining. The Treaty provided the framework for co-operation; it could not solve in advance all problems that would arise in the government of the Community.

Although the partner states cannot be criticized for looking to their national interest, they can be criticized if they accept the desirability of integration but are unwilling to accept the consequential constraints on their freedom of action. Although unhelpful, this ambiguous attitude to co-operation is nevertheless understandable. The gains from economic integration are often less obvious and longer-run than the costs and constraints. In newly independent states the politicians must necessarily be preoccupied with political consolidation and 'nation-building'. The pressure on politicians and officials alike to 'produce results' will tend to turn their attention towards national concerns, if not to the concerns of smaller areas within the nation. If co-operation between partner states is to flourish and develop under these circumstances, it is necessary for political pressure to be exerted from above. In colonial days, despite the objections of territorial governments from time to time, the continuation of the integration arrangements was ultimately assured so long as their continuation remained the policy in London. With the end of the colonial régime this force for continued integration disappeared, and a new source of pressure for integration was needed to sustain and develop co-operation.

The new force exists in the Authority, which has proved itself in the past to be able to provide the political will and leadership for integration that is required. One notable example from the past is the decision to establish the Commission on East African Co-operation at a time when relations between the three East African states appeared to have reached an impasse. Many of the problems that accumulated during the period after January 1971 might have been solved if the Authority had been meeting. Whether the political will for integration can continue to be effectively exerted if the political outlooks and attitudes to economic management and development of the partner states increasingly diverge, is however a question to which no clear answer can be given. The possible incompatibility in an economic community of the divergent policies of Kenya and Tanzania is a matter of the greatest importance for the future of the Community.

The political pressure for co-operation exerted from above is likely to be the more effective the stronger and the more active are the ministers and officials of the Community. The Community must be governed by agreement, and there is no realistic alternative to the rule of unanimity in the Councils of the Community. Nor would it be realistic to expect the partner states to devolve executive powers, for example over national planning, to the Community. But a consultative and advisory role need not make the councils and the secretariats ineffectual. The success of the Secretary-General in tiding the Community over the political crises of 1971 and 1972 suggests how great the scope would be for beneficial influence and initiative by Community officials in more auspicious times.

Any tendency for the partner states to delay and disrupt the operations of the Community in the cause of what they believe to be their national interest might be made more difficult by the generation of a stronger public belief in the possibilities of East African co-operation. The existence of such a belief is of great importance for the progress and, indeed, the survival of the Community. The troubles of the Community in the years after the signing of the Treaty, and the various barriers that were erected to free commerce and movement between the partner states, resulted in a marked cynicism about the Community among the public. The East African Ministers were seen by the Philip Commission as the channel through which Community interests would be represented within the individual national governments. They could, however, play a much wider political and educational role as spokesmen for the Community to the public of their countries. The East African Legislative Assembly could also play an important part in generating public support for continued and intensified co-operation between the partner states.

NOTES

[1] See, for example, Little, I., Scitovsky, T., and Scott, M., *Industry and Trade in Some Developing Countries* (London: Oxford University Press, 1970).

[2] Budget Speech, 1973.

[3] Ouko, R,. 'A Review of the East African Common Market in 1972', East African Statistical Dept., *Econ. Statist. R.*, June 1973, p. x.

[4] This section is based on Hazlewood, A., 'State Trading and the East African Customs Union', *Oxford B. Econ. Statist.*, May 1973.

[5] See Ouko, R., 'A Review of the East African Common Market in 1971', *Econ. Statist. R.*, June 1972, p. viii.

[6] See Hazlewood, A., 'The Co-ordination of Transport Policy', in Leys, C., and Robson, R., *Federation in East Africa* (Nairobi: Oxford University Press, 1965).

[7] Common Market and Economic Affairs Secretariat, *Review of Economic Integration Activities within the East African Community, 1973*, p, 123. See also the subsequent issue of the *Review*, pp. 148–9.

[8] Hazlewood, A., *Rail and Road in East Africa* (Oxford: Blackwell, 1964).

[9] Part of this section is based on Hazlewood, A., 'Notes on the Treaty for East African Co-operation', *East Afr. Econ. R.*, Dec. 1967.

[10] Belshaw, D. G. R., 'Agricultural Production and Trade in the East African Common Market', in Leys, C., and Robson, R., op. cit. (note 6). See also Hance, W. A., *African Economic Development* rev. ed. (London: Pall Mall Press, 1967), p. 184.

[11] Heyer, Judith, 'Review of Marketing Policies and Problems in Kenya', paper

presented to Conference of East African Agricultural Economics Society, June 1968. See also Livingstone, I., 'Production, Price and Marketing Policy for Staple Foodstuffs in Tanzania', unpublished paper for Economic Research Bureau, University of Dar es Salaam.

[12] *Report of the Select Committee on the Maize Industry* (Nairobi: Government Printer, 1973).

[13] Central Bank of Kenya, *Fourth Annual Report.*

[14] Central Bank of Kenya, *Economic and Financial Rev.*, July–Dec. 1968.

[15] See Hall, M., and Tanna, D., 'On Exchange Rate Unification: A Comment', *Econ. J.*, Dec. 1972, for an argument favouring flexibility.

10 *A Wider Community?*

(A) SCHEMES FOR A WIDER COMMUNITY

The United Nations Economic Commission for Africa had been promoting the economic integration of the Eastern African countries for
several years before the Treaty for East African Co-operation was
signed in 1967. The high point of the ECA work in this field was reached
in 1965 and 1966, when, after meetings in Lusaka and Addis Ababa,
eight countries formally resolved to establish an Economic Community
of Eastern Africa. A follow-up meeting in Addis Ababa in 1967 carried
the discussions further and examined the possible relationships between
the newly established East African Community and the wider grouping.
After that meeting the ECA initiative was not actively pursued, and the
prospects for a wider economic union in Eastern Africa centred on
the negotiations for a number of countries to become associated with
the East African Community.

(B) BENEFITS AND PROBLEMS[1]

The benefits of a wider Community in general are no different from
those of the existing Community: the economies of integration. The
economic size of the partner states and of potential new members is not
such as to exhaust economies of scale. A wider market than that of the
existing Community would be advantageous to a wide range of industries. The important question, therefore, is the extent to which the
inclusion of new members in the common market would effectively
widen the market for producers within the area.

   The unity of the East African market, it was argued in Chapter 5,
arose not only from the absence of tariffs but also from the relatively
well-developed transport facilities and the location of population and
purchasing power in relation to them. An application of the statistical
analysis reported in Chapter 5 to an area including East Africa's neighbours would give very different results. Not only are transport links

between East Africa and the neighbouring countries in general far less developed than between the three partner states. The main centres of economic activity in the neighbouring countries are remote from their borders with East Africa, and isolated from East Africa by large tracts of country in which there is very little economic development of any kind, and in many of which the potential for development is slight. In East Africa the cores of economic activity in each country are located near to their common borders. Two of the countries which have been negotiating with the Community, Burundi and Somalia, are at such a low level of economic development that they can hardly be said to possess an economic core. In the other two countries which have talked of joining the Community, Ethiopia and Zambia, the main centres of economic activity are remote from those of the partner states.

Improvements in transport between East Africa and her neighbours, and measures for economic integration themselves, could affect the locational pattern of economic activity and foster the development of the border areas. But whatever is done, it must be a long time before the 'economic distance' between East Africa and her neighbours is sufficiently reduced for a wider association to constitute an economic area as unified as that of the present Community.

If benefits would accrue from an East African common market in agricultural products because of differences in natural advantage between different parts of East Africa, it is to be expected that a wider market would yield greater benefits, because the variability of agricultural conditions is likely to be greater the larger the area. A widening of the market would therefore increase the benefit to be derived from production specialization, seasonal intra-market trade, and economies of common crop-storage. However, these benefits would be likely to be restricted in much the same way as the benefits of the common market for industry by the lack of economic unity in the wider area – to say nothing of the fact that they are not permitted to be achieved within the present Community.

It might be expected that there would still be economies of scale to be achieved in some of the common services. After all, they are relatively small concerns when seen from an international point of view, even though they are large in an East African context. In reality, the difficulties of administering the services over a much wider geographical area than at present would be likely to offset economies of scale. Indeed, the trend is towards decentralization within the existing area of their operation. Where services link countries – a new railway between a partner state and a neighbour, for example – there could, however, be advantages of joint operation, and in such a situation there might be devolution to larger units than the individual countries. Decentralization on what might be called a sub-regional basis would become feasible in a Community with more than three members, and might preserve economies of scale that would be lost in devolution to smaller units. There

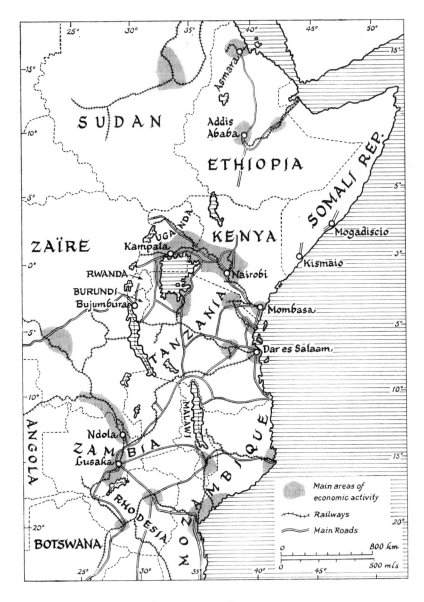

II. *East Africa and neighbouring countries*

could be advantages in raising loans for the services from guarantees by additional countries, but this would depend on the financial standing of the countries concerned.

The costs of an enlarged Community would be incurred in both its establishment and its operation. The administrative cost of the negotiations would be likely to be high because of the differences between the historical background of the East African countries and any new member. There are wide differences in institutions, in the structure of tariffs and other taxation, and in the language of government and commerce. There is nothing of the common experience that eased the negotiation of the Treaty for East African Co-operation. Zambia is closer to East Africa in these respects than the other neighbours, but even with Zambia the differences are wide. Secondly, there are the administrative costs of implementing any agreement, and implementation would be likely to involve changes not only for the new members but also for the original partner states.

The administrative costs of running an enlarged Community should also not be underestimated. The difficulty of arranging meetings among the existing three members has proved a significant obstacle to the smooth functioning of the Community institutions. The difficulty could be enormously increased by the addition of new members, unless the attitude to Community commitments among officials and ministers of the partner states changed radically, or unless the rule of unanimity in decisions was abandoned. If majority decisions did become possible in an enlarged Community the enlargement would have materially contributed to the functioning of the arrangements. Majority decisions are unacceptable among three members, but might not be so among, say, six. On balance, however, it is unlikely that the unanimity rule would be abandoned, and the enlargement of the Community would then be likely to increase considerably the burden of running the Community.

In addition to administrative costs there are, of course, the costs associated with membership of a common market which have been analysed in general terms in Chapter 2, and which are a major theme of this book with reference to East Africa. To some extent these costs can also be divided into those resulting from the establishment – the impact costs – and from the operation of the common market, but they run into each other. The success of negotiations for increased membership is likely to depend largely on the success with which arrangements are devised for minimizing the impact costs and for ensuring that the costs arising from the operation of the common market are more than balanced by the benefits flowing from it.

Finally, perhaps, mention should be made of the cost of providing the infra-structure, particularly transport facilities, necessary to make the enlarged Community an effective trading area,[2] but of course this provision would yield benefits as well as impose costs.

The possibilities for particular countries in a wider Community are

most conveniently examined with reference to those with which negotiations have in fact been carried on by the partner states. Some salient
economic facts about Burundi, Ethiopia, Somalia, and Zambia, and
about their trade with the partner states, are set out in Tables 10.1–10.4.
One point to note about the four countries is that, although each is
very different from the other, in terms of economic size and potential
Ethiopia and Zambia fall into one class, and Burundi and Somalia into
another. Both these latter countries are small, poor, and extremely

TABLE 10.1

The economies of the applicant states

	Burundi	Ethiopia	Somalia	Zambia
Area (1,000 sq. km)	28	1,241	638	752
Population (m.)	3	25	3	4
GDP (US $ m.)	205	1,395	n.a.	1,666
Proportion of GDP: percentage				
Manufacturing	7	4	n.a.	7
Mining	n.a.	..	n.a.	50
Agriculture	61	58	n.a.	6
Exports (US $ m.)	8	167	31	758
Imports (US $ m.)	30	189	45	565

NOTE: n.a. = not available.
  .. = less than ½ unit.

Sources: International Monetary Fund, *Surveys of African Economies* (Washington:
  International Monetary Fund, 1969); United Nations, *Statistical Yearbook*
  (New York: United Nations); International Monetary Fund, *Direction of Trade*
  (Washington: International Monetary Fund); United Nations, *Yearbook of Inter-
  national Trade Statistics* (New York: United Nations); Bequele, A. and Chole, E.,
  A Profile of the Ethiopian Economy (Addis Ababa: Oxford University Press, 1969).

TABLE 10.2

Exports to applicant states as percentage of exports to other partner states, 1973

	Burundi	Ethiopia	Somalia	Zambia	All applicant states
Kenya	1	4	2	16	23
Tanzania	12	1	3	42	58
Uganda	..	2	5	..	7

NOTE: .. = less than ½ unit.

Source: *Annual Trade Reports.*

TABLE 10.3

Imports from applicant states as percentage of imports from other partner states, 1973

	Burundi	Ethiopia	Somalia	Zambia	All applicant states
Kenya	..	1	1	5	7
Tanzania	..	..	..	5	5
Uganda	..	..	..	..	..

NOTE: .. = less than ½ unit.

Source: *Annual Trade Reports.*

TABLE 10.4

Exports to Zambia, other than mineral fuels and lubricants

	shs. m.		
	1967	1970	1973
From:			
Kenya	22	43	88
Tanzania	9	36	21

Source: *Annual Trade Reports.*

undeveloped. The trade of each of them with East Africa is at a minimal level (*see* Tables 10.2 and 10.3), and their failure to export to East Africa has almost certainly more to do with the absence of competitive productive capacity than with the existence of artificial barriers to trade. Tanzania's exports to Burundi, other than petroleum products, are tiny. There may be scope for mutual tariff concessions between East Africa and Burundi and Somalia, but neither can be plausibly seen as able to benefit from and ready to accept the obligations of full membership of the common market.

Somalia makes no use of the Community's surface transport system, and she has no railway to integrate with that of East Africa. Any benefits to be gained from a merger of her harbours, postal and telecommunications, and airways administrations with those of East Africa may not outweigh the administrative costs of amalgamation. Communications between East Africa and Somalia are poor, and while the desirability of improving them might be seen as a reason for Somalia's representation on the Communications Council, the limited influence of that body on road development diminishes the benefit likely to accrue from it.

Burundi is highly dependent on East African Railways and on the Harbours Corporation. Her interest is as a consumer of their services, and could perhaps be more appropriately met through a form of user representation than through membership of the corporations. It is not

likely that the addition of Burundi to the membership of the corporations would bring economies in operation or add to their status in the
eyes of international lenders.

Ethiopia is at least potentially an economy which can be seen as on a
par with those of the partner states, and a conceivable member of a
common market. However, trade is severely limited by the poverty of
the communications between East Africa and the economically more
developed parts of Ethiopia, and this would greatly restrict the effect of
any removal of artificial barriers to trade. Nevertheless, Ethiopian
membership of the common market would be potentially a significant
contribution to the formation of a wider Community. It is more difficult,
given the widely different historical and constitutional situations of
Ethiopia and East Africa, to see a merger of institutions as a matter of
practical politics.

Zambia is a different matter. The nature of her institutions is not so
different from that of East Africa's as to create major problems of integration. The considerations which cast doubt on the desirability of
membership of the corporations by Burundi and Somalia do not apply
to an economy of the size and strength of Zambia's. Her trade with East
Africa has been growing since she began her policy of turning northwards, and the trend could be greatly accelerated by the improvement in
communications brought about by the opening of the Tanzania–
Zambia railway. Membership of the common market is therefore a
matter of practical significance.

Although negotiations for the accession of new members to the Community must be undertaken by the partner states together, and any
accession to membership must be with the consent of all three, their
interests in a widening of the Community differ, and they would be
differently affected by the accession of different new members. In
general, it is to be expected that Kenya, as the most developed partner
state, is better placed than the other members to take advantage of an
enlargement of the Community. On the other hand a widening of the
boundaries of the Community would change its balance, and Kenya
might find herself less at the economic centre of the Community than
before. From this point of view, Kenya might be expected to be particularly interested in the accession of Ethiopia, and Tanzania in that of
Zambia. Kenya might feel that the accession of Zambia would encourage
a close connection between Tanzania and Zambia and a weakening of
Tanzania's links to the north. It is true that Tanzania is not tied to
Kenya in the way that land-locked Uganda is tied. Indeed, with the
transport improvements of the early 1970s Tanzania and Zambia began
to have the same kind of relationship to each other as Kenya and
Uganda, with the difference (which should give pause to any who think
that a Tanzania–Zambia link is more 'natural' and would have fewer
problems than a Tanzania–Kenya link) that Zambia has alternative
access to the outside world, and that the political circumstances which

had concealed the fact were rapidly changing in 1974, with developments in Mozambique and Angola.

An association with Zambia could however supplement rather than replace the existing links, helping them to work more smoothly. For example, in some ways separate Kenya–Uganda and Tanzania–Zambia railway systems would make more appropriate operational units than a single Kenya–Uganda–Tanzania system, though the Tanzanian Northern Line would fit best into the Kenya–Uganda system. If there is to be a drastic decentralization of East African Railways, devolution to such units would be preferable to decentralization into smaller, individual country systems. And the creation of sub-regional headquarters would promote the more equal distribution of the expenditures of the common services, which is one of the aims of the Treaty.

The change in the balance of the Community resulting from the accession of new members could in itself strengthen its cohesion. In a wider Community the strains might be more widely distributed and the discontents less concentrated. Tanzania might feel less in danger of economic domination by Kenya in a Community in which Zambia was also a member.

It would be unfortunate, and against her own interest, if Kenya adopted the mirror-image of this attitude and came to believe that she would lose from an enlargement of the Community. During the early 1970s trade between East Africa and Zambia expanded substantially. Kenya benefited most. The trade statistics need adjustment to allow for the fact that from 1974 crude oil for the newly established refinery in Zambia (not counted as an East African export, although it travels by pipe-line from Dar es Salaam) replaced the export of petroleum products from the Dar es Salaam refinery. The figures in Table 10.4, which exclude petroleum products, show distinctly the advantage Kenya was able to take of the increased scope for trade with Zambia. There is no reason to suppose that Kenya would be unable to benefit from a growth in trade arising from Zambia's accession to the common market.

(C) ADAPTING THE TREATY[3]

It may be said that while the Treaty *allows* for the accession of new partner states it does not *provide* for it. Article 93 says: 'The Partner States may together negotiate with any foreign country with a view to the association of that country with the Community or its participation in any of the activities of the Community or the Corporations.' But the Treaty is not written in a way which would make it possible for a potential new member simply to 'sign on the dotted line', even if she were prepared to accept all the obligations, and wished to enjoy all the privileges, of the original partner states.

With the passage of time various temporary provisions of the Treaty ceased to be relevant: the interim arrangements for the Distributable

Pool; industrial licensing; some provisions for quantitative restrictions on trade in agricultural produce and in goods subject to contractual obligations; the financing of the University of East Africa in the period before it was divided into separate universities. This removed some of the complications in extending the Treaty to new members. The dissolution of the East African Income Tax Department removed another. There remain many provisions of the Treaty which, because they use such expressions as 'the three Partner States', would require purely formal amendment to embrace additional members of the Community, and others in which amendments of substance would be necessary. The amendments required in the different parts of the Treaty are discussed below.

Finances of the Community

Most of the complications in the provisions for the financing of the Community had disappeared by 1974. By the middle of that year a permanent system had not been devised to replace the Treaty system, which became inoperative when the East African Income Tax Department was dissolved. Any new system would be likely to be adaptable to contain additional members, so long as they participated fully in the Community services and institutions and amalgamated their customs and excise administrations with that of the partner states.

Customs Administration

The Treaty sets out rules for attributing customs revenue to the consuming state when duty has been collected upon the entry of the goods into one partner state and they are subsequently transferred to another partner state. There is no difficulty when the customs duty is specific or when the goods are transferred in their original condition. In both these circumstances the amount of duty collected is known, and that is the amount to be passed on to the consuming country. A problem arises with *ad valorem* duties when goods are imported in bulk and transferred to the consuming country after repacking into smaller lots. It is then necessary to calculate the amount to be paid on the basis of some convention. Local costs incurred in handling and repacking are not dutiable, and allowance is made for this by providing that the importing state shall pay to the consuming state an amount equal to 70 per cent of the duty that would be payable if duty were assessed on the retail price of the goods. The 30 per cent deduction (which conforms to pre-Treaty practice) is based on estimates of the average difference between c.i.f. and retail values. It is an average around which there must be a wide dispersion for different goods and is not universally accepted within East Africa as the proper figure. There is no reason to assume that it would be the right figure to apply to transfers between the existing members of the

Community and new members. It would be possible either to recompute the average, including transfers to the new members in the calculation, or to specify different figures for different trade flows.

The existing practice could be applied to new members in the interim while more appropriate figures were being calculated, so that there would be no hindrance to the accession of new states. The Treaty allows the Authority to change the method of calculation and the amount of duty to be paid over at any time.

East African Development Bank

Although the greater part of the Charter of the East African Development Bank is of general applicability, and would not require revision if further states joined the Bank, there are some crucial provisions which in their present form have specific reference to Kenya, Tanzania, and Uganda.

First of all, however, it would need to be determined whether the Charter permits the accession of further *states* to membership of the Bank. Article 2 of the Charter allows for the admission to membership of 'any body corporate, enterprise or institution . . .' If this Article does not in fact cover the admission to membership of a state, the Charter would require revision.

Whatever interpretation may be put on Article 2, some subsequent articles of the Charter are not in a form which easily allows for membership by additional partner states. The partner states are treated differently from other members, and are given a special position in several respects in the provisions concerning the capital of the Bank. They would require amendment if new states joined the Bank. It would be logical to increase the capital if other countries joined, because such additional membership would widen the geographical scope of the Bank's activities and hence the need for funds. Articles on the subscription of the capital might need amendment as they do not envisage membership by additional states.

Article 10 of the Charter provides that the Bank may operate in the territories of the Partner States, and a new partner state would presumably automatically qualify under this Article. But Article 13, para. (*c*), lays down the allocation of the Bank's investments between the three original partner states. This distribution of the investments would need to be amended if further countries were admitted to membership, unless it was agreed to keep separate the finances of the Bank for original members and new members, and to regulate the distribution of investment between new member states in some different way.

The Charter provides that there shall be not fewer than three and not more than five directors, one being appointed by each of the three partner states. Presumably each new member state would appoint one director, and the total number would have to be increased to provide continued, and perhaps increased, representation of members who were not partner states.

The Charter of the Bank is carefully devised and its balance could be easily upset. It may be that the partner states would be unwilling to admit another country to the Bank unless and until that country has assumed the full obligations of the Treaty as a whole. On the other hand, a state wishing to be associated with the Community is likely to wish to join the Bank because of its role in fostering balanced development. The potential benefits of Bank membership may persuade an acceding state to accept obligations imposed by the Treaty of which it would otherwise be wary, and in this way the fuller integration of new states into the Community may be facilitated.

Membership of Community Institutions

The articles prescribing the membership of the various Community institutions could, by purely formal amendment, be made applicable to an enlarged Community. Such changes might none the less prove unsatisfactory if the Community were enlarged by more than one or two new partner states.

There would seem to be no alternative to enlarging the Authority by the inclusion of the Head of each acceding state. The Common Market Tribunal could be increased in size by the addition of one member for each acceding state, and it may be that the size of the Tribunal could be increased substantially before it became unwieldy. It might be desirable if an enlarged Tribunal were able to operate with a quorum of members.

Changes might need to be made in the provisions for the membership of the various councils. Each council consists of the East African Ministers together with other Ministers of the partner states. In the case of the Finance Council each state appoints one other member – the Minister responsible for finance. The same representation could be given to a considerable number of new partner states before this Council became over-large. For the other councils it is provided that each partner state shall appoint three members in addition to its East African Minister. If the membership of these councils were to be increased by four for each new partner state they might become unmanageably large if there were more than one or two accessions to the Community. Attention would also need to be given to the appropriate size of the East African Legislative Assembly.

Services Administered by the Community

If a new member were to be on precisely the same basis as the three existing partner states it would be necessary (and desirable in the interest and as an expression of the closest co-operation between the members) for its corresponding services to be taken over by the Community.

However, it does not seem an essential matter of principle that this should happen for all the services, although there are certainly some for which it would be of great importance. The substantial amendment to the Treaty would be necessary to provide for a state to operate its own customs and excise department, and there would have to be special arrangements for its contribution to the finances of the Community if it were not to participate in all the major services. In addition, so much of the Treaty, particularly of Article 20 on the transfer tax, depends on data provided by the Customs and Excise Department that it would be difficult to administer if these data were not all on a common basis and supplied from a common source. Different administrations of customs and excise, even if under identical laws, would inevitably lead to differences of interpretation and application and to a growing divergence between the practices of the different administrations. They would introduce a divisive instead of a cohesive influence into the Community.

The Corporations

The Treaty raises no formal obstacles to the amalgamation of the railways and other services of a new member with those administered for the three original partner states by the various corporations established by the Treaty, though Articles 74 and 75 would require amendment to provide for the representation of new members in the administration of the corporations. However, there would be severe practical problems in the transfer of ownership and control to the corporations, and a substantial period of time would be needed for the operational and administrative integration of the services. Nor might it be agreed that such an amalgamation should take place. The Tanzania–Zambia railway is a precedent for the provision of a service outside the administration of the Community, without amendment of the Treaty.

Consideration would need to be given to the position of a country which wished to join a particular corporation, but which had no relevant assets to bring with it – a land-locked country wishing to join the Harbours Corporation is an obvious example. The membership of the Corporation by Uganda provides a precedent, but it is not one that it would necessarily be thought desirable to apply to every new state associating with the Community.

The Treaty provides for 'strong and functionally comparable' regional headquarters of the Railways Corporation and the Posts and Telecommunications Corporation to be established in each of the three countries, and it may be expected that an acceding state would wish to be included in this arrangement. The Treaty also refers to some particular developments of the services in Tanzania and Uganda, and it is likely that an acceding country would wish for some commitments on development to be made in her favour.

A new member would doubtless wish to share in the allocation of the headquarters of the Community institutions, but the costs involved in a further reallocation, and the absolute limit set by the number of head-quarters to be located, would make it difficult to meet such a wish. It is probable that the desire for an equitable geographical distribution of the existing Community institutions would have to be met within the bounds of the policy of decentralization. However, if a new field of co-operation were established, requiring a new administration, the headquarters might be located in the territory of an acceding state.

Contractual Obligations and Agricultural Products

The general freedom from quantitative restrictions on intra-East African trade does not apply to the products listed in Annex II (contractual obligations) and Annex III (certain agricultural products). An acceding state might wish to add to the list of contractual obligations. It might wish to negotiate for additions to, and possibly for removals from, the list of agricultural products, and changes in the list could be made by the Authority at any time under Article 13.

External Trade Arrangements

Article 7 provides that 'No Partner State shall enter into arrangements with any foreign country whereunder tariff concessions are available to that Partner State which are not available to the other Partner States.' This Article would require amendment if a widened Community were to include countries which are not and countries which are in some way associated with the European Economic Community.

(D) FORMS OF ASSOCIATION OF OTHER STATES

As there can be no question of another state simply adhering to an unamended Treaty – signing on the dotted line – the difference between full membership by an additional state and other forms of association with the Treaty states is blurred. And if it is the case, as seems most probable, that even with the Treaty amended in the respects described above so as to provide for new members, no country would be prepared to make overnight the changes required to give effect to the Treaty, the distinction becomes even less clear-cut. Several gradations of association can be envisaged. At one extreme would be a form of association which merely allowed an associate the minimum adjustment-time needed before assuming the full obligations of the existing partner states. At the other extreme would be an arrangement in which the Community was associated as a unit with another state by a separate treaty, involving in some respects different principles, obligations, and institutions.

Transition to Full Membership of the Community

Even given the amendments required in the Treaty to make the accession of additional states possible it is unlikely that an acceding state could at once conform to the full requirements of the Treaty. A new member could not be expected to adopt the same external tariff as the other members overnight. She might need time to remove quantitative restrictions and tariffs on intra-East African trade. Conformity in excise duties, and in the tax-allocation arrangements, could not be achieved at once. Integration into the administrative arrangements of the Community would also require time.

Negotiations with a country applying for membership of the Community would have to result in an agreement under which the applicant would adjust its arrangements in the various spheres of Community activity to conformity with those of the partner states. Adjustments by the partner states themselves should not be ruled out, particularly as experience since the Treaty came into force has shown that the Treaty arrangements are not unchangeable. Preferably, the adjustments should take place according to a predetermined timetable, though there should be provision for flexibility in the timetable – a slowing of the agreed rate of tariff changes, for instance – under prescribed circumstances.

Transition to Partial Membership of the Community

The form and content of the Treaty were deeply influenced by the fact that the three partner states had been closely associated for many years. It is hardly to be expected that other states, not associated in the past, could readily adhere to all the provisions of the Treaty, and some countries might wish for a form of membership of the Community which required them to adhere only to those parts of the Treaty which appeared to be appropriate and relevant.

One possibility is that an applicant country would wish to join the common market but not the common services. This possibility has its attractions, for it seems to avoid the complications of associating additional states with the complicated institutional arrangements of the Community and with what might to some applicants seem to be the irrelevancies of the common services. In fact, it is not easy to isolate the common-market sections of the Treaty in this way.

There would be no difficulty in arranging for other states (given time for adjustment) to adhere to the provisions of the Treaty relating to the absence of restrictions on intra-East African trade and a common external tariff. It is unlikely, however, that a state would consider adhering to these parts of the Treaty unless it also participated in the arrangements for regulating the operation of the common market in the interest of 'balanced' development. A new member might therefore wish to participate in the transfer-tax system and the Development Bank. By participating in the Development Bank the new member would at once be involved with one of the institutional arrangements of the Treaty. But its involvement could not stop there. If the new member were to be permitted to impose transfer taxes, the other members would undoubtedly require the new member (and it would be in her own interest as well) to take part in the arrangements for supervising the operation of the Treaty and enforcing its terms. It would be necessary for the other members to be satisfied that the new member adhered to the conditions for the imposition of a transfer tax, and that the rules relating to price discrimination, barter trade, and so forth, were not broken.

It may therefore be presumed that acceding to the common market would involve acceding to the regulatory arrangements of the Treaty, which include a great deal of the institutional apparatus of the Community, from the Authority down. Membership of the Common Market Council and of the Tribunal would be essential. Membership of the Economic Consultative and Planning Council and of the Finance Council might be no less essential, the former because it might in effect be concerned with 'regulating' the Common Market by decisions affecting industrial location, and the latter because of its concern with the financing of the Community, including the institutions in which the new member would participate. Membership of the Communications Council would also be desirable because effective participation by a new member in the Common Market may depend very much on improvements in communications. Regulation of the Common Market would be greatly facilitated if the new member functioned under a common customs and excise law and administration. The new member might need to appoint an East African Minister and to have some representation in the Assembly. A viable 'partial membership' of the East African Community would be possible on this basis, but it is a membership which, even without an East African Minister and representation in the Assembly, goes well beyond a simple adherence to the 'common market sections' of the Treaty.

It is possible to visualize an arrangement under which a new member did not amalgamate its customs and excise administration with those of the original partner states, and did not participate in the associated revenue-allocation arrangements. It would, however, require very substantial amendment to the Treaty to provide means for the new member to contribute to the cost of those Community institutions (including the central secretariat) in which she did participate, and for the administration of any transfer taxes imposed by a member operating a separate customs administration.

There can be no doubt, however, that many of the common services are inessential from the viewpoint of a new member primarily interested in membership of the common market. They include the Directorate of Civil Aviation, the Meteorological Department, and numerous research organizations. But in many of these services there are notable economies of scale, and it might be very beneficial for a new member to participate. A 'partial' membership of the Community, therefore, might not stop all that far short of 'full' membership.

It might, of course, stop short of membership of the corporations. Some of these are largely irrelevant to some neighbouring countries, though by no means to all. With the reorientation of her trade northwards, East African Harbours is of very direct concern to Zambia, as also to another inland state, Burundi. The completion of the Tanzania–Zambia railway would make an amalgamation with East African Railways a possible, though not by any means a necessary development. There might be advantages to be obtained from the geographical extension of the postal and telecommunications and airways administrations, though the difficulties might predominate.

The other possibility must not be ignored, that a country might wish to participate in some of the activities of the Community, including one or more of the Corporations, but not in the common market. The importance of the improvement of communications, particularly for some countries, before a wider common market could be an effective vehicle for the expansion of trade, makes it understandable that a country might think that association with the transport activities of the Community should have priority over membership of the common market. Or a country which was a user of the Community transport services might wish for an association which gave it some say in their administration, without wishing to undertake the obligations of membership of the common market.

For the original partner states, however, there is an important connection between the common market and the common services, which must make them cautious about the idea of 'partial' membership of the Community. The joint operation of the common services, including the Corporations, and their financial arrangements, are part of a 'package' which includes the common market. The acceptance of the Treaty by a partner state may have resulted from the calculation that, although it got less (more) out of the common-market agreement, this was balanced by the fact that it got more (less) out of the common services. The concept of partial membership abandons the idea of a 'package' in which there is a balancing of the more and the less beneficial elements of the Treaty, and opens the way for serious difficulties between the original partner states. If a new member were to be allowed to pick and choose between those obligations of membership which it does and which it does not wish to accept, it might be asked why a similar privilege should be denied to the original partner states. But to allow a partner state to opt out of those parts of the Treaty it finds less beneficial than others would be a recipe for rapid disintegration of the Community.

Association on Special Terms with the Community

A country might wish to participate in the common market yet not be prepared to accept the precise conditions specified in the Treaty for the operation and regulation of the market.

It might wish, for example, to exclude some commodities (for the time being) from the requirement to impose no tariffs or quantitative restrictions on intra-East African trade; it might wish to impose a higher rate of transfer tax than is permitted under the Treaty, or to enjoy less restrictive conditions in other ways on the use of transfer taxes; it might wish for some special consideration because of difficulties imposed by a low level of industrial development in its exporting to the rest of the Community. It might be open to a new member to negotiate different contributions towards the cost of the common services. Under the Treaty arrangements the three countries contribute in proportion to certain of their tax revenues. A particularly poor country acceding to the Community might wish to contribute less than in proportion (on the analogy of a progressive tax system). A country which participated in only some of the services would also not wish to contribute to the same extent as a country which participated in them all.

As most, if not all, neighbouring countries are less industrially developed than the three partner states it is indeed likely that they would wish to negotiate less stringent rules of membership, and the partner states might be prepared to accept association on such less stringent terms as a stage in the establishment of a wider common market in which the associated countries would in time achieve identical conditions of membership.

Association with the Community on Different Principles

There may be no way of associating another country with the Community by amending the Treaty if that country finds one or more of the fundamental principles of the Treaty unacceptable. It may, none the less, be possible to accommodate a beneficial association of such a country with the Community within a separate treaty.

A country's unwillingness to surrender autonomy in tariff policy, and an insistence on retaining the right to determine import duties unilaterally, would indicate an unwillingness to accept a basic principle of the Treaty. There may be scope for associating such a country with the Community in a free-trade area.

Possibly the most important principles about which there could be differences of opinion are those concerning the regulation of the common market. It may be that some countries would wish for more specific and powerful measures for the co-ordination of industrial development within the wider common market than are provided under the principles of the Treaty. For other potential associates of the Community fiscal transfers might be more appropriate than either the regulatory mechanisms of the Treaty or other measures for regional industrial planning that might be introduced. The need for fiscal compensation might be strongly felt by a country whose public revenues suffered substantially from its joining the common market, and whose prospects for industrial development, inside or outside the common market, were not great. Either through amendment of the Treaty or through an *ad hoc* arrangement a system of fiscal compensation could be introduced. By the relevant time the partner states might have made progress towards a planning solution of their trade and development problems. Nevertheless, countries which attached particular importance to these instruments might feel that their requirements could be best met under a new treaty, and the partner states might agree.

It might also be desirable to envisage a limited form of association for countries which could not be expected in the reasonable future to attain full membership of the Community. Such an association might include a limited free-trade area, not necessarily with formal full reciprocity when the associate was a much less-developed country than any of the partner states. It might provide the associate with membership of a users' council for the transport services of the Community. This device might be appropriate when the use of the services was important for the associate but the partner states thought full membership of the corporations was inappropriate.

It would be right for the partner states to leave open the possibility of various forms of association. But it is of vital importance that no form of association should damage or detract from the integrity of the Community of the three partner states.

(E) PROSPECTS FOR A WIDER COMMUNITY

Although other countries have expressed interest in association, formal and substantial negotiations have been conducted only with Burundi, Ethiopia, Somalia, and Zambia. The negotiations began in November 1968 at Mombasa, where meetings were held between the East African Negotiating Team and ministerial delegations from each of the applicants. Two features of the form of the negotiations should be noted. First, on the East African side the responsibility for the negotiations is with a team of Ministers of the partner-state governments and not with the Community. This arrangement results from the fact that the Treaty provides not that the Community but that 'the Partner States may together negotiate with any foreign country'. Secondly, the negotiations are with each applicant separately, and not with the four applicants as a group. The widely different circumstances of the different applicants probably makes it essential to carry on the negotiations separately, and to accept differences in the terms of association of the different applicants. There could, in principle, be difficulties about the relations between the applicants themselves after any agreement is reached between East Africa and one or more of them separately, but as their economic links with each other are slight the problem should not be serious.

Very little has been made public about the progress of the negotiations, although it is known that the different applicants have been seeking different relationships with the Community.[4] It is also known that no formal negotiations at ministerial level have taken place since 1970, so that it may be presumed that the enlargement of the Community is not imminent. It may be surmised that at the time of their original approaches to the partner states the applicants were not well informed about the nature of the Community, nor had they fully evaluated the benefits they would obtain from association. With further understanding of the Community, and a closer look at the advantages of association, they may have had second thoughts. This could be one of the reasons for the slow progress of the negotiations. But in addition, political events in the applicant countries must have diverted their attention to internal matters. It would be unrealistic, for example, to expect that in 1974 Ethiopia would be giving much attention to her economic relations with East Africa. And events in East Africa and the problems of the Community institutions cannot have increased the attractiveness of an association to other countries.

Though there are no indications that the partner states have been responsible for the failure of the negotiations to progress, political developments in some of the applicant countries (for example, the rumoured increasing military strength of Somalia, with the resulting dangers in any revival of the border issues between Somalia and Kenya) may not have increased the attractiveness of association to one or more of the partner states.

It was suggested above that the circumstances of the four countries are such that Zambia alone could be a potential candidate for full membership of the Community within a foreseeable period of time. But this is to say nothing of Zambia's wishes. Whatever Zambia's intentions at the time of her original approach to East Africa, political changes in Portugal in the middle of 1974, and the probable consequential changes in the status of Angola and Mozambique, could have relieved much of the pressure she felt for a reorientation of her economy towards the north, and deflated her interest in association with the Community.

This chapter has emphasized the difficulties of enlarging the Community and has minimized the benefits. It may, indeed, seem strange that the question of enlarging the Community is under consideration at all at a time when there can be serious doubts about the ability of the Community to cope with its existing responsibilities. Although the negotiations for enlargement of the Community have not been effectively pursued for some years, if the Community survives the difficulties of the 1970s the possibility of the accession of new members, or of other forms of association of neighbouring countries, must not be ruled out. The immediate economic gains from a widening of the Community might be small, for all parties, but they would be likely to grow. The possible political advantages of a concrete expression of African unity, in the form of a wider association, should also not be ignored. What can be said with certainty is that the chance of reaping benefits from a widening of the Community depends on the existing Community first putting its own house in order.

NOTES

[1] Discussions of wider Eastern African integration are to be found in Massell, B. F., 'Industrialization and Economic Union in Greater East Africa', *East Afr. Econ. R.*, Dec. 1962, and *East African Economic Union: An Evaluation and Some Implications for Policy* (Santa Monica: The RAND Corporation, 1963) chap. V; Ndegwa, P., *The Common Market and Development in East Africa* (Nairobi: East African Publishing House, second edn 1968), chaps. 7, 8, 11; and O'Connor, A. M., 'A Wider Eastern African Economic Union? Some Geographical Aspects', *J. Modern Afr. Studies*, 1968, No. 4.

[2] For some orders of magnitude see Hazlewood, A., and Tresidder, J. O., 'Transport and Regional Development in Africa', *Civil Engineering Problems Overseas 1971* (London: The Institution of Civil Engineers, 1971), pp. 249–50.

[3] This and the following section are based on Hazlewood, A., 'The Kampala Treaty and the Accession of New Members to the East African Community', *East Afr. Econ. R.*, Dec. 1968.

[4] See Byalugaba, J. M., 'Wider Association on the Cards', *African Development*, Feb. 1974, East African Community Special Survey, p. 25.

11   *The Future?*

In the second half of 1974 many could be found who would doubt if the Community had a future. One of the corporations had been in total disarray, and although the outlook had brightened it remained unclear. The Authority had not met for four years, and no material progress was being made on many questions of great consequence for the integration of East Africa. The Community might, indeed, be seen at best as stagnating and at worst as crumbling into dissolution. A new Secretary-General, it is true, had assumed office without difficulties, the post passing in the proper order from a Kenyan to a Tanzanian. There were signs that the Common Market Tribunal was at last coming into active existence. But these were small things to set against the evidence for the disruption of the Community. Those who looked to the past could see that co-operation in East Africa had survived crises that seemed at the time to be as severe, but it would have been rash to assume that the appearance of imminent collapse would always prove deceptive.

However, it should be said that the tensions of the time must be judged against the recent history of East African integration. The years from 1965 to 1970, the years of the formulation and implementation of the Treaty, saw a great forward stride in co-operation between the three countries. It should not be unexpected that a period of such rapid change and innovation should be followed by a time of relative stagnation, and even of a resurgence of tensions between the partner states. This should be even less surprising when it is remembered that the new integration arrangements were introduced during the early years of independence and nation-building for each of the partner states, when the constraints of co-operation must have seemed particularly onerous, the constraints of colonialism having so recently been overcome.

What of the self-interest of the partner states? Had anything occurred since 1967 to diminish the material benefits of co-operation? If at that time the Treaty provided an acceptable, though finely balanced, distribution of perceived benefits, then the growth of the East African economies in the ensuing years should have increased the attachment of the partners to the Community. The gains from the common market at the time of the Treaty were generally believed to be modest because the level of industrial development was low. An improvement in the efficiency of a small sector of the economy cannot make more than a small improvement in relation to the total. But with the growth of the manufacturing sector (see Table 11.1), and with the increased importance within the

TABLE 11.1

Manufacturing and repairing as percentage of GDP in monetary economy

	1967	1971	1972
Kenya	15	16	16
Tanzania	10	14	14
Uganda	7	13	n.a.

NOTE: n.a. = not available.

Source: EASD, *Economic and Statistical Review.*

sector of industries which possess economies of scale, the benefits of the common market should increase both absolutely and relatively. If the common market was acceptable in 1967 it should be acceptable, *a fortiori*, in 1974 and 1980.

This acceptability should be reinforced by the consideration that the constraints of co-operation are likely to be less restrictive than those imposed by the lower level of income and development that would be the consequence of non-co-operation. The alternative to co-operation should not be seen as simply an increase in the governments' freedom of action, but also the lower level of income that would result from the loss of the economies of integration.

The pressure for continued co-operation exerted by the existence of perceived benefits depends, however, on there being no radical change in the distribution of the total East African benefit between the partners. But an unchanged distribution cannot safely be assumed in a changing economy. It has already been remarked that the Treaty was a 'package deal' which gave to the different partner states different things. It is probable, for example, that Tanzania accepted less than she thought she deserved in the way of an improved distribution of the benefits of the common market because she recognized the benefits she obtained from the common services, particularly the transport services, in which it was generally acknowledged that there was a cross-subsidization in favour of Tanzania. But if the value of the items in the package changes, or if it is believed to have changed, the acceptability of the package will also change.

It was said in Chapter 8 that a belief in Tanzania that the pattern of cross-subsidization in the railways had changed to her detriment may

have been partly responsible for the suggestions that she was withdrawing from the Railways Corporation. In other words, the value of this
item in the package had changed, so that the acceptability of the package
had changed. The likelihood of such changes makes it necessary for the
Community to be flexible. One cannot all the time be re-negotiating the
Treaty, but there is likely to be a need from time to time to find ways
within the general framework of the Treaty for adjusting the operation
of the Community to meet any radical changes in the distribution of the
benefits of integration. Such adjustments would be easier to achieve if
economic planning played a greater part in regulating the relationships
between the partner states than was acceptable at the time of the Treaty.

The failure of the Kampala Agreement was perhaps too recent for the
Philip Commission to think that planning was practicable as a regulator
of the common market. The Treaty established a market regulator, the
transfer tax being the main device for influencing market forces in the
desired direction. It appears probable, however, from what was said in
Chapters 7 and 9, that the market mechanism, as influenced by transfer
taxes, will not be effective in preventing the establishment of an
excessively high-cost industrial structure through the duplication of
plants in which economies of scale are large in relation to the market of
any one partner state. Planning may be required, therefore, not only to
influence the location of industry but also to limit the uneconomic
multiplication of producing plants. Without the adoption of a planning
solution to the problem there is a serious danger of the consolidation of
high-cost industrial structures in each of the partner states.

The need for planning suggested by this argument is reinforced by a
consideration of the effect of the common market on the industrialization policies of the individual partner states. There is a strong deterrent
against a partner state deciding that the benefits which would flow from
local production of a particular product would not justify the high costs
that would be involved. A partner state reaching such a conclusion
would very probably find that the industry would be set up in another
partner state, and that sufficient protection would be accorded the
industry in the course of a 'package deal' at the discussions which take
place between the partner states in preparation for the annual budgets.
The first of the partner states would then have the costs of protection
without any of the benefits of the industry: it would be better if the
industry were not established at all. It is the worst of both worlds to
have the industry in another partner state: the partner state establishing
the industry receives its benefits, whereas the costs are partly borne by
the others. There is, therefore, an incentive for a partner state to jump in
first and to establish an industry before it is established elsewhere in
East Africa even though for the Community as a whole the costs outweigh the benefits. In this way the common market is a formula for the
establishment of increasingly high-cost industries and for an increasingly
protective structure of tariffs and quotas. In time there may be a reaction

against the high costs imposed by the common market and reflected in the highly protective tariff, and the common market may disintegrate.

The dangers of an excessive level of protection have already become apparent in East Africa: tariffs on some products were reduced in 1973 and 1974, and it was agreed to examine the implications of a general reform of the tariff.[1] In itself, a lowering of protection could merely increase the competitiveness of imports and reduce the developmental influence of the common market. Accompanied by a planned rationalization of production, and specialization agreements offering economies of scale, it could raise the efficiency of East African industry and preserve the benefits of the common market while reducing its costs.

There are other elements of the situation less concerned than the role of planning with the principles of the Treaty, but none the less important, that must be tackled if pressures for withdrawal from the Community are to be deflated. Of particular importance is the state of crisis that from time to time engulfs one or other of the corporations. If the Railways Corporation, to cite one that was in extreme difficulties in 1974, is unable to carry the traffic offered to it because it cannot afford the spares to maintain its equipment, and if it cannot pay its headquarters workers, Kenya at least, being the country most affected, is likely to feel that she could do better on her own. If Kenya finds her nationals in the employment of the railways in Kenya unpaid, and she decides to guarantee the payment of their wages herself, as she did in July 1974, and as earlier in 1974 she 'bailed-out' the Railways Training School, she will not for long believe that the benefits of an East African railways administration outweigh the costs. She may be mistaken in such a conclusion, because it is not obvious that a Kenyan railways administration would be immune from the management difficulties of the East African Corporation. But decisions on such matters as the level of the tariff and the pattern of capital expenditure would be within the competence of the government of Kenya, without the agreement of the other partner states being necessary. The dissolution of so major a component of the Community as the Railways Corporation would mean a serious contraction in the role of the Community in the economy of East Africa, and would deprive the Community of an instrument for the pursuit of the development and equalization aims of the Treaty.

Another matter, not to be ignored just because it is not concerned with fundamentals, is the petty squabbling that recurrently sours the atmosphere of co-operation. This particularly concerns employment. A newspaper reported in March 1974:

Kenya's Railway African Union yesterday forced the removal of four Tanzanian employees of the East African Harbours Corporation from the port of Mombasa. The action was taken in retaliation for Kenyans allegedly being prevented from taking up promotion posts in the Corporation's headquarters in Dar es Salaam.[2]

More generally, it was suggested that

> Within the EAC itself, there are petty officials and other employees
> who hardly think East African, while their actions are basically
> parochial . . . One subtle reason for such a state of affairs is the fact
> that many employees of the Community have failed to appreciate the
> difference between 'indigenisation' of employed manpower in their
> respective territorial sectors and 'East Africanisation' of the services
> rendered by the Community.[3]

Reference may be made in the same context to such irritants in inter-
state relations as the alleged decision of Kenya to hold back transfers of
funds to the Harbours Headquarters in Dar es Salaam in retaliation for
the alleged failure of Tanzania to transfer funds to the Railways Headquarters in Nairobi. In this connection, to understand is not to forgive.
Unless such bickering becomes a less prominent feature of Community
affairs one may come to doubt the partner states' commitment to the
Community.

Commitment may be encouraged by pressure from outside institutions
such as the World Bank, which has large sums invested in the corporations, for which the partner states are 'jointly and severally' responsible.
But a unity based on the 'leverage' of aid donors would be a very fragile
thing.

Much more important than the bickering and squabbles between the
partner states is the growing gap between their economic and social
philosophies. Differences between the partner states can always occur as
a result of chance events. The hostility between Uganda and Tanzania in
1971 may be so categorized and, it must be admitted, provides an argument in favour of market-oriented integration, rather than mechanisms
in which governments play a more positive part. These differences,
which make it difficult for the Authority to meet and to play an active
role, can lead to stagnation, and worse. But of more fundamental
concern, and more open to rational examination, is the compatibility
within the Community of countries pursuing such widely different
social and economic philosophies as those of Kenya and Tanzania.

There is not room here to elaborate the differences. It is perhaps
sufficient to say, it is hoped without caricature, that Kenya is committed to the 'acquisitive society', and increasing the role of native
Kenyans within it, whereas Tanzania aims to pursue the path of self-
reliance and socialism.

One individual Tanzanian's view of the common market is that

> it did almost nothing to encourage long term development for it
> merely served to open up East Africa to much more effective exploita-
> tion by foreign capital while doing nothing to solve the basic cause of
> our poverty . . . we cannot proclaim the creation of a customs union
> as a progressive step forward if it has the effect of sinking us even
> further into the abyss of poverty and degradation or if it necessitates
> compromising our policies of Socialism and self-reliance.[4]

The writer concludes that 'meaningful common markets and meaningful federations can only be constructed on the basis of an ideology which is in large measure common to all participant states'.

This is an unnecessarily gloomy conclusion. It may be argued that the divergence of ideology within East Africa makes federation out of the question. It may also be argued that total economic union would not be feasible unless the conditions existed which would also permit political association. Even if these two arguments are accepted the question of the compatibility of a more limited degree of economic co-operation with divergences of ideology remains open, particularly as it is easy to exaggerate the influence of ideology on the policies actually pursued.

Certainly, economic integration would be difficult to operate in some fields if policies were widely different. It is difficult, for instance, to envisage the practicability of a common central bank, but that is a field of integration the possibility of which had already been abandoned before the Treaty, for reasons unconnected with differences in ideology. Freedom of capital movements does not seem a likely candidate for an integration scheme in which one country is pursuing socialist policies. But freedom of capital movements was not guaranteed by the Treaty. Policies required by a particular social philosophy can add to the difficulties of integration. Tanzania's regional policy, under which it is attempted to spread economic development more evenly throughout the country, might increase the difficulty of equalizing development between the partner states: the equalizing mechanisms which might attract an enterprise to locate in Dar es Salaam or Arusha rather than in Nairobi, might not be strong enough to achieve its location in Dodoma. The implementation of radical domestic policies may overburden the administration and distract attention from Community affairs. But economies of scale are independent of ideology, and they will continue to be available in the foreseeable future, if they are not offset by administrative inefficiency, through East African co-operation, and only through East African co-operation. This fact may, despite ideology and domestic distractions, persuade the partner states that co-operation is worth while.

If the Community is to survive into the 1980s positive decisions will be required of the partner states. The review of the transfer-tax system provided for by the Treaty did not take place, and the system continued as before. 'Muddling through' will not be enough next time. The Treaty provides that its common-market sections 'shall remain in force for 15 years after coming into force and shall be reviewed by the Partner States before the expiry of that period' (Article 92). Unless arrangements for the common market are reviewed and renegotiated in time it is not just the regulatory innovations of the Treaty that will come to an end in December 1982; the common market itself will cease to exist. It remains to be seen whether the feeling for East African unity and the benefits of co-operation will carry the Community on to and beyond that crucial date.

NOTES

[1] See Kenya 1973 and 1974 Budget speeches, and speech by Community Minister for Common Market and Economic Affairs, EALA, June 1974, para. 89.

[2] *Daily Nation* (Nairobi), 23 March 1974.

[3] loc. cit., 25 March 1974.

[4] Nsekela, A. J., *African Development*, Feb. 1974, East African Community Special Survey, p. 17.

Postscript

Chapter 11 looked at the future of the Community as it appeared during the second half of 1974. After a further six months had passed the outlook was darker: the clouds had accumulated and the occasional rays of sunshine were less easily detected. In March 1975 the integration arrangements in East Africa seemed to be in a deeper crisis than ever before.

The common market provisions of the Treaty were virtually a dead letter. The scarcity of foreign exchange was seen by the governments as the overriding problem, to the solution of which the benefits of the common market and free inter-state trade were a necessary sacrifice. Quantitative restrictions on inter-state trade were so commonly applied that they had ceased to arouse protests. The Common Market Tribunal existed in form, all its members having at least been appointed, but there seemed little purpose in pursuing cases when violations of the Treaty were so obvious and widespread.

The outstanding event affecting the trade of a partner state had been the imposition of restrictions on the growing road traffic between Kenya and Zambia. At the beginning of December, Tanzania imposed severe restrictions on heavy vehicles transporting goods between Kenya and Zambia. The grounds for the restrictions were that the vehicles were damaging the roads. The view in Kenya was that this was an excuse, and that the restrictions were imposed out of jealousy of Kenya's success in the Zambian market, at a time when Tanzania was looking to a strengthening of her own political and economic ties with Zambia. Whatever the truth of the matter, the effect of the restrictions was to bring nearly to an end a promising development in Kenya's export trade.

These restrictions on the use of the roads led to strained relations between Kenya and Tanzania expressed in acrimonious debate in press and parliament. Kenya herself closed some border roads, stating that road works made them impassable, there was interference with rail traffic, and Kenya interrupted steamer traffic on Lake Victoria, ostensibly because of an outbreak of cholera. At the same time a squabble developed over the alleged expulsion of Kenyans from Tanzania, which added to the ill feeling between the two partner states.

The situation in the corporations had also worsened by the early months of 1975. The publication of the report of a Select Committee of the East African Legislative Assembly on malpractices in the Harbours Corporation was expected in May; it was rumoured that the report would recommend the dissolution of the Corporation as a common service. It was being said that the transfer of revenues from Kenya to the Dar es Salaam headquarters was not taking place, and that the Kenyan and Tanzanian harbours were in effect being operated as separate enterprises.

The most striking development in the common services, however, had been in the Railways Corporation, which in February 1975 had discontinued its passenger services in Kenya and Uganda. The agreement of July (*see* p. 100) under which the governments were to make payments to the Corporation had not been implemented, and there was again a failure to transfer revenues from the regions to headquarters. The financial difficulties of the headquarters had prevented them from maintaining the stock of spare parts, and the closure of the passenger services was the consequence. Dissension between the partner states was exacerbated by the fact that the Tanzanian Government had itself purchased spares for use in Tanzania, where the passenger services continued in operation.

The closure of the passenger services in Kenya and Uganda was only the most dramatic manifestation of the continuing problems of the Corporation which had not been successfully tackled. The consultants brought in after the July meetings had been able to achieve nothing. At the beginning of March 1975 the Communications Council had agreed to a further increase in railway charges, but it seemed unlikely that this would make more than a marginal contribution to the solution of the Corporation's troubles.

The increasing dissension between Kenya and Tanzania had led some to believe that the Community would soon disintegrate, and that Tanzania would seek other associations, particularly with Zambia. In fact, the prospect of such an association replacing that of the partner states looked less likely than it had in the past. Zambia had not taken kindly to the disruption of her trade with Kenya, from which she had gained exports as well as imports, and it seemed unrealistic to imagine that with the completion of the Tanzania–Zambia railway Zambia would necessarily be eager to embrace a Tanzania separated from her East African partners. It was more plausible to expect that with changes in Mozambique, more friendly relations with Malawi, and the possibility of political developments in Zimbabwe, Zambia's interest in the north would cool. In that event, it seemed that the potential advantages of existing association might come to loom larger in Tanzanian eyes.

But however indistinct the future, it was crystal clear that renewed life could be breathed into the Community only by a decision at the highest political level. The Authority, despite rumours circulating in the middle of 1974 that a meeting was imminent, still had not convened by March 1975, and there was no talk of its doing so. The idea that a new look at the integration arrangements was necessary was being increasingly canvassed. To agree that there was such a need is not to admit the failure of the Treaty. The environment of co-operation had not remained static since the signing of the Treaty. It was not to be expected that, in a changing situation, provisions for all time could have been laid down in 1967. The Treaty did foresee the need for a review of the transfer tax system, and that was already long overdue. The foreign exchange difficulties of the partner states were far more severe than they had been when the Treaty was drawn up. One obvious matter for examination was the possibility of devising measures which would make restrictions on the use of foreign exchange compatible with the development of interstate trade. Equally obvious was the need for a new look at the financial and administrative arrangements of the corporations. This is not the place to catalogue all the issues requiring attention. Suffice it to say that unless decisions were soon taken to re-examine the issues in a spirit of partnership, and with the political will to agree, the outlook for the Community looked bleak. It might formally survive – the strength of self-interest in a preservation of the administrative structure should not be underestimated – but survive in a state of inanition in which it was unable to provide the benefits of integration and co-operation its founders sought.

Index